SO-AFS-033

Gem Selection

Scottish Songs

Edited by
ALFRED W. TOMLYN
Mus. Bac.

Scotpress
Bruceton Mills, West Virginia
1988

First published by Valentine & Sons Ltd.

Reprinted 1984 by
SCOTPRESS
P.O. Box 397
Bruceton Mills, WV 26525

Second Impression 1988
ISBN 0-912951-09-5
Printed in USA

Printed by Morgantown Printing & Binding Co.
Morgantown, WV USA

INDEX

NOTES

Caller Herrin' (p. 1).

The words were written by Caroline, Baroness Nairne, *née* Oliphant (1766–1845). Born and died at Gask House, Perthshire; married (1806) William Nairne, heir to the attainted title of "Baron Nairne," to which he succeeded in 1824. Lady Nairne in her last years co-operated with Dr. Chalmers in philanthropic work. She was one of the most charming of Scots poetesses. The air was composed by Nathaniel Gow (1766–1831)—son of the great Neil Gow, and father of Neil Gow, jun.—who was born near Dunkeld, attained great skill as a violinist, became one of his Majesty's trumpeters for Scotland (1782) and "leader" of many of the Edinburgh concerts in the early decades of the nineteenth century. He was afterwards a music publisher in the Scots capital, where he died. The air is said to have been suggested to him while listening to the curious harmony amid discord produced by the sound of the bells of St. Andrew's Church, Edinburgh, mingling with the street cries of the fishwives vending their wares.

Annie Laurie (p. 4).

Written by William Douglas of Fingland in honour of Anne, youngest daughter of Sir Robert Laurie of Maxwellton, Dumfries. The date of the song may possibly be assigned to the close of the seventeenth century, owing to the fact that Laurie was not created a baronet until 1685. Mr. Douglas owed several suggestions to an old version of "John Anderson, my Jo," to the tune of which song his own was sometimes sung. The song was later somewhat changed by Lady John Scott, who composed the air to which it is now sung, and re-wrote some of the verses to suit the melody.

Logie o' Buchan (p. 6).

George Halket (1690?–1756), schoolmaster of the parish of Rathen, Aberdeenshire, was the author of the words of this popular song. Halket was a zealous Jacobite, and wrote several satirical lyrics, one of which has been preserved, viz. "Whirry, Whigs, awa', Man." So incensed was the Duke of Cumberland with one of Halket's pieces—"A Dialogue between the Devil and George II."—that he offered £100 for the body of the song-writer, living or dead. But Halket could take care of himself. As regards the *locale* of "Logie o' Buchan," it is situated in Crimond, the parish adjoining Rathen, while "Jamie," who to his industry as a delver united skill "on the pipe and the viol sae sma'," was the laird's gardener, James Robertson. The air is said to be adapted from that to which the craftsmen of the Tailors' Corporation were wont to march—"The Tailor fell through the Bed, Thimbles an' a'."

There was a Lad was Born in Kyle (p. 7).

In this song Burns very aptly describes his own temperament and career, one verse being almost prophetic in its appropriateness to his case, viz. "He'll hae misfortunes great and sma'," &c. The poet was well able to gauge his own greatness, and had too little of the humbug in him to affect ignorance of it, therefore he could write without the faintest suspicion of boasting, "We'll a' be proud o' Robin," and give the date of his birth, 25th January 1759. The air was taken from that of an old pre-Reformation song, "O gin ye were dead, guidman," which John Knox and the Reformers adapted to a popular hymn of the time.

Duncan Gray (p. 9).

Words by Robert Burns (1759–96), while the air is traditionally credited to a Glasgow carter bearing the same designation as the hero of the song, Duncan Gray, who is said to have written it early in the eighteenth century. Burns wrote the piece for Thomson's "Collection of Scottish Songs," basing it upon an older song which he had written while at Mauchline, and which in turn had been suggested to him by the ancient popular "catch":—

> "As I cam' in by Aberdeen
> Hech, hey, the girdin' o't."

Comin' thro' the Rye (p. 10).

Of this song only the first four lines are by Burns, the remainder being the work of John Walter, a musician in Edinburgh, who later became a music-seller there, but eventually migrated to London. Burns, as is well known, wrote a complete song under this title, basing it on an old lay, the coarseness of which infected his own strain. Published in Johnson's "Museum," it achieved some measure of popularity, but the humour and sentiment were both so tinged with vulgarity that Burns's version was superseded by Walter's, which some writers even ascribed to Burns. The air was a very ancient one, known as "The Miller's Daughter," but was modified by Walter to suit his words.

Auld Robin Gray (p. 11).

The words of this lyric, undoubtedly one of the most exquisite in the whole range of Scottish verse, are by Lady Ann Barnard, *née* Lindsay (1750–1825), eldest daughter of the Earl of Balcarres and wife of Sir Andrew Barnard, Secretary to the Governor of the Cape Colony. Her ladyship was so charmed with an old air, "The Bridegroom Greets when the Sun gaes doun," that she wrote her song to be sung to it. For some time it was so sung, until the Rev. W. Leeves (1748–1825), rector of Wrington, Somerset, composed the tune with which it is now generally associated.

Mary of Argyle (p. 13).

This exquisite lyric is the work of Mr. Charles Jefferys, author of several well-known songs, "The Rose of Allandale," "Jeannette and Jeannot," &c., and was written about 1850. The melody was composed by Sidney Nelson, a popular musician of that time.

Cam' ye by Athole (p. 15).

Of this song, whose popularity is surpassed by few, the words were written by James Hogg

(1770–1835), the Ettrick Shepherd, being published in an ephemeral publication, "The Border Garland," while the air was the composition of Neil Gow, jun. (1795–1823), the grandson of the great violinist.

Within a Mile o' Edinburgh Toun (p. 17).

Singularly enough, though this song seems to smack of Scottish soil, neither the words nor the music are of Scots origin. Of the former, the brilliant humorist and wit, Tom D'Urfey (1630–1723), whose "Pills to Purge Melancholy" still serve to accomplish their somewhat coarsely expressed mission, may be said to be the author, the present form of the piece being an adaptation of his "'Twas within a Furlong of Edinburgh Town," published in Playford's "Wit and Humour" (1798). The air is the work of James Hook (1746–1827), the father of the celebrated wit, novelist, and *improvisatore*, Theodore Hook.

The Flowers o' the Forest (p. 18).

There are two versions of "The Flowers o' the Forest," each referring to different circumstances, or rather disasters. Both are beautiful, though the charm is of a different type in each. Of the version here given, the words were written by Mrs. Cockburn of Ormiston, *née* Alison Rutherfurd (1710–94), the sentiment being inspired by the financial ruin which had overtaken the families of some neighbouring landed proprietors. The air is a modernised adaptation of an old tune.

Afton Water (p. 20).

Few songs are better known or oftener sung than this, of which the words are by Burns (written in 1786) and the melody by Alexander Hume (1811–59). The lady, to whom the lyric was inscribed by our great national singer, was Mrs. General Stewart of Stair and Afton, on whose estate, Afton Lodge (beautifully situated on the stream whence it takes its name, and which is a tributary of the Nith) are located the scenes described in the song. She was the first person to publicly recognise the genius of Burns.

Green Grow the Rashes O! (p. 22).

Still another song by Burns, while the air is very ancient. It first appears in a mutilated form in Oswald's first Collection (1740), but previous to that it had been long known, being used as a reel as well as a song. In the MS. Lute-Book of Sir R. Gordon of Straloch (1627) occur the two airs "Grene grews ye Rasses—A Daunce" and "I kist her quhile shee Blusht," which on comparison are found to be almost the same.

Scots Wha Hae (p. 23).

This noble lyric, which may almost be styled the "National Anthem" of Scotland, was written by Burns during a period of great imaginative exaltation and excitement. In company with his friend Syme he was riding from Kenmure to Gatehouse-in-Fleet (Galloway) by a moorland road, where the more rugged and gloomier aspects of nature predominated. The sky suddenly became overcast and lowering, the wind moaned across the desolate waste, and a thunder-storm of terrific violence began. Burns really enjoyed the awful spectacle; "The fine frenzy" of the poet came upon him, and amidst the fury of the elements "Scots Wha Hae" came into existence. The air to which the words were originally written was, "Hey, Tuttie Tattie," traditionally stated to be the march which Bruce ordered to be played before Bannockburn to inspire his troops with the hopes of victory. True, Thomson and others have repudiated such an idea, and actually induced the poet to write a second set of verses adapted to the tune "Lewie Gordon," which they considered more akin to the spirit of the piece than "Hey, Tuttie Tattie." One thing is certain, that the latter air is very ancient, having certainly been sung to Alexander Montgomery's (1545-1610) "Hey, now the Day Dawes" in the *Gude and Godlie Ballatis*, which in turn is said to have been an adaptation of a still earlier song. Later in the history of Scotland the tune was seized upon by the Jacobites as a capital air for their favourite "Here's to the King, Sir," and is printed as such in Hogg's *Jacobite Relics* (Vol. I. No. lxvi.).

Wae's Me for Prince Charlie (p. 24).

Words by William Glen (1789-1826), a Glasgow merchant, while the air, which is entitled "Johnnie Faa, or The Gypsie Laddie," appeared in Johnson's "Museum" (1789-90), being there set to an ancient ballad recounting an elopement which is alleged to have occurred in the grand old Scots family of Cassillis when the Ladye Jean eloped with "Johnnie Faa, the Gypsie Laddie." The air appears under a modified form in the Skene MS. (1630), being there entitled "Ye Ladye Cassylis Lilte."

Bonnie Dundee (p. 26).

The words of this fine lay were written by Sir Walter Scott (1771-1832), being intended for his historical melodrama, "The Doom of Devorgoil," published in 1830. The air is anonymous, but the late Sir Herbert Oakeley maintained it must have originated, though perhaps suffering certain later modifications, with the Jacobite rising of 1715. He stated he had evidence to prove it was in existence in 1740. Alas, he has been removed before making public the ground of his belief!

Jock o' Hazeldean (p. 28).

Words also by Sir Walter Scott, being believed to be founded on the old ballad "Jock o' Hazelgreen." The first verse is a remnant of an older piece, but the succeeding stanzas are all from the mint of the great poet's fancy, and the song as a whole was contributed to Alexander Campbell's (1764-1824) publication, "Albyn's Anthology" (1816). As regards the air it is undoubtedly ancient, appearing in the Leyden MS. (1690) under the title "The Bony Brow," which is to be preferred to "Willie and Annet" upon which the later setting is based.

The Laird o' Cockpen (p. 29).

From the pen of the Baroness Nairne (*vide supra*, p. v.) came the words of this exceedingly popular lyric of which the charm never seems to fade. The prototype of the "Laird o' Cockpen," who was prood and great, with "his mind ta'en up wi' the things o' the State," was a devoted adherent and bosom friend of Charles II., who accompanied the monarch into exile. At the Restoration, however, he was overlooked, and his estates, of which he had been deprived by Cromwell, seemed lost for ever. But obtaining permission one day to supply the organist's place in the Chapel Royal, he suddenly introduced, in place of the " Dismission Voluntary," the air "Brose and Butter," of which the king had been very fond in his exile. Charles recognised the tune, called for his old favourite, and reinstated him in his lands. Originally, the song ended with the refusal of the Laird. Miss Ferrier, however, added two stanzas in which she described "Mistress Jean's second Thoughts" and her acceptance of her "canny suitor." The air is very old, having been regarded as ancient even in 1709 when it appeared in the Crockat MS., being set to the seventeenth century song, "When she cam' ben she bobbit."

The Land o' the Leal (p. 31).

This is unquestionably the finest lyric in the Scots vernacular, with the exception of one or two of Burns's best. The words are by Lady Nairne, while the air, which is identical with that associated with "Scots Wha Hae," though set in different time, is, as we have seen, very old.

Ye Banks and Braes o' Bonnie Doon (p. 32).

This is another of Burns's noblest lyrics, being written for Johnson's "Museum" (1790), although there was an older version, "Ye Flowery Banks o' Bonnie Doon," inspired by the sad fate of a young Ayrshire lady who died of a broken heart on being deserted by her lover. Tradition says the air is Irish, but Burns specifically states that it was composed by Mr. James Miller, writer in Edinburgh, under circumstances as extraordinary as they were romantic. (See Burns's "Letters to Thomson.")

John Anderson, my Jo (p. 33).

Burns wrote the words, basing them upon an earlier version which appeared in MS. about 1560, "John Anderson" being, as was currently reported, the town-piper of Kelso. The first verse of the older song ran as follows :—

" John Anderson, my jo, cum in as ze gae bye,
  And ze sall get a sheep's heid, weel baken in a pye,
  Weel baken in a pye, and the haggis in a pat ;
  John Anderson, my jo, cum in and ze's get that."

The air is also of considerable antiquity, dating back at least to 1630.

The Rowan Tree (p. 35).

Another fine lyric by Lady Nairne, obviously written out of the depths of her own experience in connection with the scenes of her girlhood. It originally formed one of her "Lays of Strathearn." The date of the air is unknown, but some authorities have ascribed it to Corelli.

Come Under my Plaidie (p. 36).

Of this beautiful song, Hector M'Neill (1746-1818) was the author, a man whose genius was fitted to achieve greater things than he ever accomplished had he but learned the lesson of the conservation and concentration of intellectual force. This song, also written for Johnson's "Museum," presents to us a vivid drama in real life, being founded on incidents coming within the personal knowledge of the poet. The composer of the air was John MacGill, a native of Girvan, Ayrshire, who was celebrated in his day as a violinist of no mean skill. Besides composing the airs of several songs, he wrote reels, strathspeys, &c., which were of note in their day.

Gloomy Winter's Noo Awa' (p. 38).

The author of the words of this very popular song was Robert Tannahill (1774-1810), the well-known Scottish song-writer, who for tender pathos and the expression of the softer emotions was only excelled by Burns. Born in Paisley, the son of a hand-loom weaver, he received but a scanty education before he was called on to enter the same vocation, at which he laboured until his death at the early age of thirty-six, pursuing poetry with assiduity in his spare hours. The air to which it is customarily sung is styled in Neil Gòw's "Fourth Collection of Reels, &c.," "Lord Balgonie's Favourite : a very old Highland tune." This opinion is questioned by Stenhouse in the Notes to Johnson's "Museum" (1787-1803), who states that Mr. Alex. Campbell, editor of "Albyn's Anthology," had asserted it to be of modern origin. It certainly appears in a very scarce publication, "The Countess of Eglinton's Collection," about 1740, but in a slightly different form to what is known to us to-day.

The Bonnie Banks o' Loch Lomon'
(p. 40).

The pathos and charm of this lovely lyric, with its air so suited to the expression of the mournful sentiments it declares, are if anything heightened by the discovery of the fact that we know nothing regarding the composition of either. The origin alike of words and melody is wrapped in obscurity, tradition only venturing the guess that the song referred to the hardships and sufferings endured by the Jacobites after the failure of the Rebellion of 1745.

Robin Adair (p. 42).

Of this song the authorship is unknown, while the tune is claimed respectively by England, Scotland, and Ireland. The claims of Scotland have, however, been favoured by the best-informed critics. As a lyric it is literary and a musical gem.

Of a' the Airts the Wind can Blaw
(p. 43).

The words of this song are by Burns, being written about 1790 for Johnson's "Museum." Difference of opinion exists as to whether he wrote it all, some critics affirming that he only wrote the first two quatrain stanzas, John Hamilton, the musician and music-seller, being credited with the second pair, and William Reid, bookseller in Glasgow, with the third pair. But Cunningham's theory that Burns wrote the whole poem, while Hamilton and Reid merely revised some of the lines to adapt them to the air, is finding acceptance. Reid, however, *did* write some verses of his own to sing to the tune, but they are distinct altogether from those given in our text, and begin :—

> " Upon the banks of flowing Clyde
> The lassies busk them braw."

The air to which Burns wrote his words was an adaptation of "The Lowlands o' Holland" as it appeared in Johnson's "Museum," the adapter being Mr. William Marshall (1748–1833), the Duke of Gordon's house-steward, and was styled by him, "Miss Admiral Gordon's Strathspey."

My Nannie's Awa' (p. 45).

Another of Burns's choicest lyrics, instinct with pure grace alike of form and sentiment. It was written in 1794 for the "Collection of Scottish Airs" edited by George Thomson (1757–1851). Of the origin of the exquisite melody with which it is wedded, nothing can be discovered.

There's nae Luck aboot the Hoose
(p. 46).

Considerable controversy has been waged regarding the authorship of this song, one set of critics assigning it to William Julius Mickle, of Langholm (1734–88), the author of the ballad of "Cumnor Hall," and the translator from the Portuguese of Camoens' *Lusiad ;* while another section ascribed it to Jean Adams (1710–65), a schoolmistress of Crawford's Dyke, near Greenock. Evidence exists which might cause it justifiably to be assigned to either. It first appeared in Herd's "Collection" (1766), was then sung in the streets as a ballad (*cir.* 1771), and finally obtained a place in all the collections published towards the close of last century. The words may have been revised by Dr. Beattie, and certainly the sixth stanza proceeds from his pen. The air to which the song is sung was based on an old Jacobite melody "Up an' waur them a', Willie," which dates back to the Rebellion of 1715. (Hogg's "Jacobite Relics.")

My Love she's but a Lassie yet
(p. 48).

To the beautiful air associated with this song, no fewer than three sets of words can be sung, viz. those by Burns ; second, those by Hogg ; and the ballad, "A Famous man was Robin Hood," based on Wordsworth's well-known poem. Hogg's version is by some preferred to Burns's. The first quatrain is :—

> " My love she's but a lassie yet,
> A lightsome, lovely lassie yet ;
> It scarce wad do to sit and woo
> Down by the stream sae glassy yet."

In the early song and dance books the tune is known as "Lady Badenscott's Reel."

Roy's Wife of Aldivalloch (p. 49).

The song is the production of Mrs. Grant, of Carron (1745–1814), but who is not known to have written any other lyric. The air was of old called "The Ruffian's Rant," and was a favourite with Burns, who wrote "Can'st thou leave me thus, my Katy?" to it.

Wandering Willie (p. 51).

The words are written by Robert Burns, and appeared in Thomson's "Collection" (1793), while the air was published in Oswald's "Caledonian Pocket Companion" (1750–55).

Scottish Blue Bells (p. 52).

The author of this song was Charles Doyne Sillery (1807–36), son of a captain in the Royal Artillery, and after failing to obtain entrance to the Royal Artillery, successively turned his attention to a naval career, then to the study of medicine, thereafter to the life of a man of letters, and finally to the Church. He died, however, in his twenty-ninth year, of consumption. He wrote several poems and many songs, some of them of no small promise. The air was composed by George Arthur Barker (1812–76), a vocalist of great repute in his day, who also wrote many songs, the "White Squall" being the best known.

The Bonnie Brier Bush (p. 54).

With regard to this song it is the air which has tempted the song-writers to adapt words to it, not the words attracting the composers. The melody in its earliest form is undoubtedly very ancient, but it has been frequently adapted. The oldest version of the song is very rude, so much so that Burns largely re-wrote it, and contributed it to Johnson's "Museum" along with the air to which he had adapted the words. Then Lady Nairne, dissatisfied with the ending of Burns's version, still further modified his modification of the old piece, also suiting the words to the melody. Both Tannahill and Robert Gilfillan prepared versions, and Messrs. Parlane, of Paisley, in their "National Choir," published a third, but none of these have attained the popularity of Lady Nairne's adaptation of Burns.

My Heart is Sair (p. 55).

This plaintive lyric was written by Burns for Johnson's "Museum," adapting to the purpose one of Ramsay's songs in the "Tea-table Miscellany," entitled "For the Sake of Somebody." The air is old, and was originally adapted to a four-line stanza in place of one of eight lines as here.

The Birks o' Aberfeldy (p. 56).

The words are by Burns, who is said to have written them while visiting the Falls of Moness near Aberfeldy in Perthshire, utilising for his purpose an old tune, "The Birks o' Abergeldie" published in Playford's "Dancing Master" in 1657. Musicians will note the peculiarity in this melody, that throughout, the note *fah* of the scale is entirely omitted.

Mary Morison (p. 58).

Though this song was one of Burns's earliest lyrical efforts and was somewhat undervalued by himself, so competent a critic as William Hazlitt has pronounced the opinion, with which most readers will agree, "that it takes the deepest and most lasting hold on the mind." The air to which it was originally sung was "Bide ye Yet"; but that has been long since exchanged for the one called "The Miller," which appeared in Johnson's "Museum," and is remarkable for the pathetic sweetness of its final cadence.

Ca' the Yowes to the Knowes (p. 59).

Of this song Burns wrote two versions, the earlier seemingly being founded on an old song taken down by the poet from the singing of a clergyman. In a letter to Thomson, Burns said, "When I gave it (the old song) to Johnson, I added some stanzas and amended others, but still it will not do for you. In a solitary walk to-day, I tried my hand on a few pastoral lines following up the idea of the chorus, which I would preserve. Here it is with all its crudities and imperfections on its head." The result is the exquisite pastoral lyric as we now have it. The melody, which is pre-eminently suitable to the verse, also partakes of the Doric or pastoral character. It was somewhat modified by Burns.

Flora Macdonald's Lament (p. 61).

James Hogg, the Ettrick Shepherd (*q.v.* p. vi.), wrote the words of this exquisite dirge, appending the following note: "I got the original of these verses from my friend Mr. Neil Gow, who told me they were a translation from the Gaelic, but so rude that he could not publish them, which he wished to do on a single sheet for the sake of the old air. On which I versified them anew, and made them a great deal better without altering one sentiment." In another note prefixed to the song in "Hogg's Works," in the volume "Songs" (1831), the following intimation is made: "This was composed to an air handed me by the late lamented Neil Gow, jun., who said it was an ancient Skye air, but afterwards told me it was his own."

Bonnie Wee Thing (p. 63).

Words by Burns, the subject of his praise being Miss Davies, whom the susceptible poet styled "My little idol, the charming lovely Davies." Of her Allan Cunningham also wrote that "her education was superior. . . . She was equally agreeable and witty, her company being much courted in Nithsdale." Burns penned another song in her praise, viz. "Lovely Davies," which appeared in Johnson's "Museum." Alas, through a disappointment in love she died of a broken heart! The air, evidently borrowed from Oswald's "Caledonian Pocket Companion" (1750–55), is probably adapted from the air of the song, "Wo betyd that wearie Bodie," contained in the Straloch MS. (1627–29). See Irving on "Scots Music."

A Man's a Man for a' That (p. 64).

Few songs written by Burns have attained the lasting popularity of this. It is one of those that laugh at the lapse of years. The French Béranger says of it: "This song is not one for an age, but for an eternity." The more the pity that it was the means of marring the career of Burns in the Revenue Service, for, in those days, to utter sentiments in favour of popular freedom was equivalent to writing oneself down a cut-throat and a French Republican. The air, the origin of which is very ancient, contains features characteristically Scots.

O Whistle an' I'll come to ye, my Lad (p. 65).

Words by Burns, and singularly enough he wrote two versions of this song, one of which appeared in Johnson's "Museum," and the other in Thomson's "Collection." By many critics the air has been assigned an Irish origin, because set to a song, "Since Love is the Plan, I'll Love if I can," which has a place in the opera "The Poor Soldier," written by John O'Keefe, and produced at Covent Garden (1783). But despite this it was written by a Dumfries violinist, John Bruce, about the year 1750. Burns vouches for its authorship in a letter to Thomson, from Dumfries: "Bruce, who was an honest fellow, though a *red wud* Highlander, constantly claimed it, and by all the old musical people here he is believed to be the author."

Kate Dalrymple (p. 67).

The words were written by William Watt (1793–1859), a somewhat eccentric genius who dabbled in painting, poetry, and music. He wrote many songs—which were so numerous as to be collected in a volume—also psalm tunes, reels, &c., and acted as precentor in East Kilbride Parish Church. Some of his other songs, "Hab o' the Mill," "The Tinkler's Waddin'," "Katie Christie," are still popular. The air, which is of great antiquity, appears in an altered form in Johnson's "Museum," being there set to "I hae been at Crookieden" (to wit, the infernal regions); but prior to that time it was known as "Jinglin' Johnnie."

The Hundred Pipers (p. 69).

The words of this stirring song are by Lady Nairne, the incidents whereon she based it being as follows. When Prince Charles Edward occupied Carlisle, he marched in preceded by a hundred pipers. The crossing of the Esk took place not on the march into England, but on the retreat from it. The air is evidently an ancient Scottish "catch" adapted by Lady Nairne herself to the requirements of her verse.

Kelvin Grove (p. 72).

The song now under consideration was written by Thomas Lyle (1792–1859), born in Paisley, and died in Glasgow, who, amid the "pauses" of a busy existence as a medical man in the Western metropolis, found refreshment and relaxation in cultivating the Muses. A volume of his " Collected Poems and Songs " appeared in 1837, and in that " Kelvin Grove " was published. The melody dates back to the early years of the eighteenth century, when it was sung to words, the title of which even is too coarse for our modern ideas.

Jessie, the Flow'r o' Dunblane (p. 73).

One of the most popular of Scots lyrics, the words of it were written by Tannahill (see p. viii.), while the air was composed by Mr. R. A. Smith (1780–1829), the son of a weaver, and who from being a weaver himself became one of the most admired composers of Scots music of his time, also precentor in the Abbey Church, Paisley, and afterwards musical conductor in St. George's Church, Edinburgh. His chief works were " Anthems for the Organ or Pianoforte " (1819) ; " Select Melodies " (1827), " The Scottish Minstrel " (1829), and " Sacred Music " (posthumous). It may interest readers to know that " Jessie " never existed outside the poet's fancy, and that Tannahill appended the last verse of his song against the advice of Smith.

Thou Bonnie Wood o' Craigielea (p. 75).

Another lyric by Tannahill, instinct with true pathos and sympathetic tenderness. The music was composed by James Barr, of Tarbolton (1770–1836), upon whom Tannahill wrote the following epigram :—

" There's blithe James Barr from St. Barchan's town,
When wit gains a kingdom, he's sure o' the crown."

Macgregor's Gathering (p. 77).

Words written by Sir Walter Scott for Alexander Campbell's " Albyn's Anthology " (1816). The subject of the piece was the virtual proscription of the clan Macgregor, by Act of Privy Council (1603), when those bearing the surname were ordered to change it, the pain of death being denounced against any who should call themselves Gregor or MacGregor. By a subsequent Act (1613) death was denounced against any of the tribe formerly called Macgregor, who should presume to assemble in greater numbers than four. The places referred

to in the song were the familiar haunts of the clan. The beautiful air to which the words are set was adopted by Alexander Lee (1802–51), a well-known singer and composer of the period, who with his wife were to be found on all the best concert platforms. Lee not only wrote many original pieces, but adapted others. The original of this air was of great antiquity, but was modernised by him.

The Boatie Rows (p. 80).

Words written by John Ewen (1741–1821), born at Montrose, went to Aberdeen and engaged in business, amassing eventually a snug fortune, which he left to charities to the exclusion of his only daughter, who, however, got the will set aside. The song appears in Johnson's " Museum," being set to no fewer than three different airs, but only one of these is now sung.

Corn Rigs are Bonnie (p. 82).

The words of this song were adapted by Burns from a very old " lilt," which goes back to the early years of the seventeenth century, commencing

" O corn riggs and rye riggs
And corn riggs are bonnie."

The air is also ancient, being of English origin, and was composed in 1680 to one of D'Urfey's songs, " Sawney was tall and of noble race." Allan Ramsay (1686–1758) was the next to utilise it, and wrote the lyric in the Gentle Shepherd, " My Patie is a Lover gay " (1725). Gay (1688–1732) then chose it for one of the songs in his opera of Polly (1729), and finally it finds a place in Adam Craig's " Collection " (1730).

O Nannie, wilt thou Gang wi' me ? (p. 84).

From the pen of Bishop Percy (1728–1811), of Dromore, the words of this lyric come, therefore it can scarcely be styled a Scots song. Burns, however, considered it the finest ballad in the language. It first appeared in Dodsley's " Miscellany," being printed " O Nancy, wilt thou go with me ? " The air was composed by Thomas Carter (1730–1804). Both words and music were in existence prior to 1773, in which year they were sung at Vauxhall by Vernon, the vocalist.

When the Kye Comes Hame (p. 86).

The words are by Hogg, who somewhat humorously apologises for the grammatical error in associating the plural "kye" with a singular verb. The tune is adapted from the old air of "The Blaithrie o't."

Will ye no Come Back Again (p. 88).

The words of this, one of the most touching and beautiful of Scots lyrics, were written by Lady Nairne, the theme being the wanderings and final escape of the young chevalier, Prince Charles Edward. From Culloden to Invergarry, from there to South Uist, thence to Skye and to Inverness, exposed to hunger, distress, and deadly peril, with £30,000 put on his head, he nevertheless bore up through all until he was able to embark at Moidart for France. To the last the fidelity of his followers was incorruptible. The air is assigned to Neil Gow, jun., and is admirably adapted to express the profound pathos of the parting scene.

The Auld Hoose (p. 89).

Also the work of Lady Nairne, the subject being the "Old House of Gask," where she was born and where she died. It was beautifully situated near the river Earn, and was associated with many episodes in the fortunes of the Jacobite party. The air was composed by Nathaniel Gow, but was unquestionably modified by Lady Nairne, who was an accomplished musician.

O Willie brewed a Peck o' Maut (p. 91).

The words are by Burns; the three friends were William Nicoll (*cir.* 1760–97), who was one of the classical masters in the Edinburgh High School, and afterwards laird of Laggan; Allan Masterton (1750–1800), writing-master in the same institution; and the poet himself. The occasion was the "house-warming" of the mansion house of Laggan (1789), and the composer of the charming air to which the song was sung was Masterton himself. The air in question has been superseded by a more modern one, evidently adapted from the older melody.

O why left I my Hame (p. 92).

The words of this lyric were written by Robert Gilfillan (1798–1850), born in Dunfermline, served apprenticeship to a cooper in Leith, was afterwards clerk in several places of business, and finally was appointed collector of police rates in Leith (1837). In the year 1831 he published a volume of "Original Songs," from which this song is taken. The air, which was also utilised by Burns in "Of a' the Airts the Wind can Blaw," was composed by Peter MacLeod (1797–1859), and seems to be adapted from "Lowlands of Holland."

Gae bring to Me a Pint o' Wine (p. 94).

Burns gives a very interesting account of the incident which suggested to him the words of this song, viz. on witnessing at Leith pier the farewells exchanged between a young officer and his lady-love on the eve of his embarkation for service abroad. The half of the first stanza is older than Ramsay's "Tea-Table Miscellany." The air is credited to James Oswald in the "Caledonian Pocket Companion," being issued *cir.* 1742. Burns's edition reads, "Go fetch to me," not "Gae bring."

The Lea Rig (p. 96).

Words by Burns and entitled "My ain kind Dearie, O," being based on an old ditty bearing the name "The Lea Rig." Of the original only one verse is extant. No fewer than three other song writers wrote versions of this old lay, viz. Fergusson, William Reid, and Lady Nairne, but that of Burns is the only one that has retained its popularity. The air was published under the title of "The Lea-Rig" in James Oswald's "Caledonian Companion."

Scotland Yet (p. 97).

To Henry Scott Riddell (1797–1870) we owe the words of this beautiful song. Born at Sorbie in the Vale of Ewes, Dumfriesshire, the son of a shepherd, he too was led to adopt the same calling. His education, therefore, was scanty; but after the death of his father he went to school, then to college, finally becoming a minister of the Church of Scotland at Teviothead. Nine years later, however, ill-health compelled him to retire from active duties, and he became a pensioner of the Duke of Buccleuch, engaging in literary work as he was able. The air was composed by Peter M'Leod (1797–1859), whose volume of "National Melodies" was exceedingly popular in its day, containing as it did songs by Fergusson, Scott, Riddell, Gilfillan, Hogg, Allan, and others, set to music in most cases by M'Leod himself. It may interest our readers to know that this song first appeared as a "broad sheet," upon which were given both the words and music, the intention being to devote the proceeds to enclose the Burns monument, Edinburgh, with a parapet and railing. This object was amply realised.

O Wert Thou in the Cauld Blast (p. 99).

The words of this charming lyric are by Burns, and a pathetic interest attaches to them, in that they were penned on his death-bed. To Miss Jessie Lewars, sister of one of the poet's colleagues in the Revenue service, the lyric was addressed, and was Burns's only possible recompense to her for her noble and self-denying offices when Mrs. Burns was laid up, in daily expectation of her confinement, and was unable to attend on her dying husband. The song found a place in Thomson's "Collection." The air often associated with the words is styled "Lochiel's awa' to France," but Mendelssohn's setting, which is here given, is now much more popular.

Castles in the Air (p. 101).

The words of this song, which was such a favourite of Thomas Carlyle, were written by James Ballantine (1808–77), who, after serving his apprenticeship as a house-painter, devoted himself to the art of painting on glass. To such eminence did he attain, that by public competition he gained the commission to illustrate the windows of the House of Lords. He was also known as a constant contributor to literature, particularly to the publication *Whistle-Binkie* (1832–53), in which appeared many of his pieces; also he published "The Gaberlunzie's Wallet," "The Miller of Deanhaugh," and other poems of high merit. The present

song is taken from the "Gaberlunzie's Wallet," and the air to which it is sung is a modification of the old melody "Bonnie Jean o' Aberdeen."

My ain Fireside (p. 103).

Words by Mrs. Elizabeth Hamilton (1758–1816), authoress of the once popular Scots novel, "The Cottagers of Glenburnie." The air to which it is sung is called "Toddlin' Hame," under which name it appeared in Johnson's "Museum" (1787–1803), though it was also known as "Armstrong's Farewell" and "The Days o' Lang Syne."

Highland Mary (p. 104).

Words by Burns. The theme of the piece was his betrothal to Mary Campbell, a girl of great beauty, modesty, and high principle, who lived as a domestic servant near Mauchline. She was a native of Dunoon, her father being one of the sailors on board the revenue cutter stationed at Campbeltown. Allan Cunningham thus writes of her: "Burns soon found she was the lass whom he had long sought but never before found . . . she saw by his looks he was sincere : she put full trust in his love, and used to wander with him among the green knowes and stream banks . . . till the moon rose, talking, dreaming of love and the golden days which awaited them. He was poor, but they resolved to wed, and exchanged vows of constancy and love. They plighted their troth on the Sabbath to render them more sacred ; they made them by a burn where they had courted, that open Nature might be a witness ; they made them over an open Bible to show they thought of God in this mutual act, and when they had done they both took water in their hand and scattered it in the air, to intimate that as the stream was pure so were their intentions." They then parted, never to meet again. She went to visit her relatives to prepare for her marriage, and died suddenly of fever. She was buried in Greenock West Churchyard. The air, "Catharine Ogie," to which the song is sung is very old, being known as far back as 1680, when it was sung at a concert at Stationers' Hall.

Lochnagar (p. 106).

The words are by Lord Byron (1788–1824), while the composer of the melody was Mrs.

Patrick Gibson (1784–1838), the wife of a well-known Edinburgh artist and art-critic, who published "Etchings of Select Views in Edinburgh" (1818). Mrs. Gibson was connected with Sir Walter Scott.

Ilka Blade o' Grass (p. 108).

The words of this popular lyric are by James Ballantine (see p. 30), who wrote them almost on the spur of the moment, on being told the story of a poor woman who had opened a shop in a certain village, and who, on a neighbour saying he feared there were already too many shops of the kind there, replied: "Ah, but Providence is kind; every blade o' grass carries its ain drap o' dew." The air, which is entitled "Sweet Dawns the Morn," is an old one, and was fitted to the words by Mr. D. R. Hay.

To Mary in Heaven (p. 109).

Words by Burns, the subject being the same as that treated of in "Highland Mary"—the poet's love for Mary Campbell—being written on the anniversary of her death, in September 1789. The air is not much older, if any. It was styled "Donald," and was probably composed towards the close of the eighteenth century, appearing in Shield's opera, "The Highland Reel," in 1788. In Thomson's "Collection" it was set to the song "From Thee, Eliza, I must go," and has also done like service with regard to other lyrics.

Auld Lang Syne (p. 111).

The words, as we have them, may be said to be by Burns. There was an old song, "Au'd Lang Syne," dating back to the early seventeenth century, which Ramsay included in his "Tea-Table Miscellany." He first cobbled the lines, then Burns almost wholly rewrote them in the immortal form in which we now have them. The first two stanzas, however, still show traces of the original. The air now always sung to the lyric was called "I fee'd a lad at Michaelmas," and was associated with it by George Thomson. The two are now indissolubly united.

Caller Herrin'.

Words by
LADY NAIRNE.

Music by
NATHANIEL GOW.

1. Wha'll buy caller her _ rin'? They're bonnie fish and halesome far_in'; Buy my caller her_rin', New

drawn frae the Forth. When ye were sleep_ing on your pillows, Dreamt ye aught o' our puir fellows

Dark_lin' as they face the bil_lows, A' to fill our woven willows, Buy my caller her _ rin', They're

bon_nie fish and hale-some far_in', Buy my cal_ler her_rin', New. drawn frae the Forth. Cal_ler

ad lib. *p*

her _ rin', Cal_ler her _ rin'.

f colla voce *p*

2. An'
3. Noo

when the creel o' her_rin' pass_es, La_dies clad in silks and la_ces,
nee_bor wives. come tent my tell in', When the bon_nie fish ye're sel_lin'

Ga_ther in their braw pe_lis_ses, Toss their heads and screw their fa_ces;
At a word be aye your deal_in', Truth will stand when a' things fail_in';

Buy my Cal_ler her_rin', They're bonnie fish and halesome fa_rin'; Buy my Cal_ler her_rin', New

1. drawn frae the Forth. **2.** drawn frae the Forth. 4. Wha'll buy my Cal_ler her _ rin'? They're

cresc.

no brought here with_out brave dar _ in', Buy my Cal _ ler her _ rin', Ye

lit_tle ken their worth. Wha'll buy my Cal_ler her _ rin'? O ye may ca' them vul_gar far_in',

dim.

Wives and mith-ers maist des-pair - in', Ca' them lives o' men. Cal - ler

ad lib. *p*

her - rin', Cal-ler her - rin'.

Annie Laurie.

Andante moderato.

PIANO

Maxwellton braes are bon-nie, Where ear - ly fa's the dew, And its
Her brow   is like the   snawdrift, Her neck is like the   swan,   Her
Like dew on the gow - an   ly - ing, Is the fa' o' her fairy   feet;   And like

there that An _ nie Lau _ rie, Gie'd me her pro _ mise
face it is the fair _ est, That e'er the sun shone
winds in sum _ mer sigh _ ing, Her voice is low and

true, Gie'd me her pro _ mise true, Which
on— That e'er the sun shone on, And
sweet— Her voice is low and sweet. And she's

ne'er for _ got shall be, And for bon _ nie An _ nie Lau _ rie I'd
dark blue is her e'e; And for bon _ nie An _ nie Lau _ rie I'd
a' the world to me, And for bon _ nie An _ nie Lau _ rie I'd

lay me doon and dee.
lay me doon and dee.
lay me doon and dee.

Logie o' Buchan.

Words by
G. HALKET.

1. It's Lo-gie o' Buchan, It's Lo-gie the laird, He has ta'en a-wa' Ja-mie that
2. Tho' San-dy has ous-en, has gear and has kye, A house and a hadden, and
3. My dad-dy looks sulky, my min-nie looks sour, They flyte up-on Ja-mie be -
4. I sit on my creepie and spin at my wheel, And think on the laddie that

delv'd in the yard; Wha play'd on the pipe and the vi-ol sae sma', He has ta'en a-wa'
sil ler for-bye; Yet I'd tak' my ain lad wi' his staff in his hand, Be - fore I'd hae
cause he is poor; Tho' I lo'e them as weel as a daughter should do, They're no half sae
lo'es me sae weel; He had but ae saxpence, he brak' it in twa, And gied me the

Ja-mie, the flow'r o' them a'. He said,"Think nae lang, las-sie, tho' I gang a -
San-dy wi' hous-es and land. Saying "Think nae lang, las-sie, tho' I gang a -
dear to me, Ja-mie, as you. Saying "Think nae lang, las-sie, tho' I gang a -
half o't when he gaed a - wa. Saying "Think nae lang, las-sie, tho' I gang a -

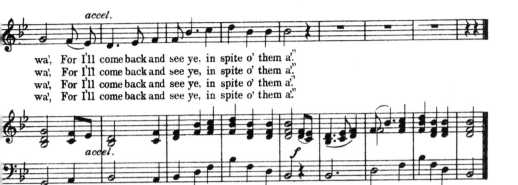

wa', For I'll come back and see ye, in spite o' them a'."
wa', For I'll come back and see ye, in spite o' them a'."
wa', For I'll come back and see ye, in spite o' them a'."
wa', For I'll come back and see ye, in spite o' them a'."

5.

Then haste ye back, Jamie, and bide na awa',
Then haste ye back, Jamie, and bide na awa',
The simmer is comin', cauld winter's awa',
And ye'll come and see me in spite o' them a'.
Ye said, Think nae lang, lassie', *etc.*

There was a lad was born in Kyle.

BURNS.

1. There was a lad was born in Kyle, But what_na day or what_na style, I
2. Our monarch's hindmost year but ane Was five-and-twen_ty days be_gun, 'Twas
3. The gos_sip kee_kit in his loof, Quo' she, wha lives will see the proof, This
4. He'll hae mis_for_tunes great and sma, But aye a heart a _ boon them a'; He'll

doubt it's hard—ly worth the while To be sae nice wi' Ro — bin. For
then a blast o' Jan—war' win Blew han—sel in on Ro — ·bin. For
wa — ly boy will be nae coof, I think we'll ca' him Ro — bin. For
be a cre — dit till us a', We'll a' be proud o' Ro — bin. For

Ro — bin was a rov—in' boy, A ran — tin', rov — in', ran — tin', rov — in',
Ro — bin was a rov—in' boy, A ran — tin', rov — in', ran — tin', rov — in',
Ro — bin was a rov—in' boy, A ran — tin', rov — in', ran — tin', rov — in',
Ro — bin was a rov—in' boy, A ran — tin', rov — in', ran — tin', rov — in',

Ro — bin was a rov — in' boy; O ran — tin', rov — in' Ro — bin.
Ro — bin was a rov — in' boy; O ran — tin', rov — in' Ro — bin.
Ro — bin was a rov — in' boy; O ran — tin', rov — in' Ro — bin.
Ro — bin was a rov — in' boy; O ran — tin', rov — in' Ro — bin.

5.

But sure as three times three mak' nine,
I see by ilka score and line,
This chap will dearly like our kin',
So leeze me on thee, Robin.
For Robin was a rovin' boy, *etc.*

Duncan Gray.

BURNS.

1. Duncan Gray cam' here to woo, Ha, ha, the woo-in' o't; On bly the Yule night, when
2. Duncan fleech'd, an' Duncan pray'd, Ha, ha, the woo-in' o't; Meg was deaf as
3. Time and chance are but a tide, Ha, ha, the woo-in' o't; Slight-ed love is
4. How it comes let doc-tors tell Ha, ha, the woo-in' o't; Meg grew sick as

we were fu', Ha, ha, the woo-in' o't. Mag-gie coost her head fu' heigh,
Ail-sa Craig, Ha, ha, the woo-in' o't. Dun-can sigh'd baith out an' in,
sair to bide, Ha, ha, the woo-in' o't. "Shall I, like a fool", quo' he,
he grew hale, Ha, ha, the woo-in' o't. Something in her bos-om wrings,

Look'd a-sklent, and un-co skeigh, Gart poor Dun-can stand a-beigh,
Grat his een baith bleard an' blin', Spak' o' loup-ing o'er a linn,
"For a haught-y hiz-zie dee? She may gae to-France-for me!
For re-lief a sigh she brings; And, O! her een, they spak' sic things,

Ha, ha, the woo_in' o't.
Ha, ha, the woo_in' o't.
Ha, ha, the woo_in' o't.
Ha, ha, the woo_in' o't.

5.
Duncan was a lad o' grace,
Ha, ha, the wooin' o't;
Maggie's was a piteous case,
Ha, ha, the wooin' o't.
Duncan couldna be her death,
Swelling pity smoor'd his wrath,
Now they're crouse and canty baith,
Ha, ha, the wooin' o't.

Comin' thro' the Rye.

ANONYMOUS.

1. Gin a bo_dy meet a bo_dy Comin' thro' the rye, Gin a bo_dy kiss a bo_dy,
2. Gin a bo_dy meet a bo_dy Comin' frae the town Gin a bo_dy meet a bo_dy,
mang the train there is a swain, I dearly lo'e mysel'; But what his name, or whaur his hame, I

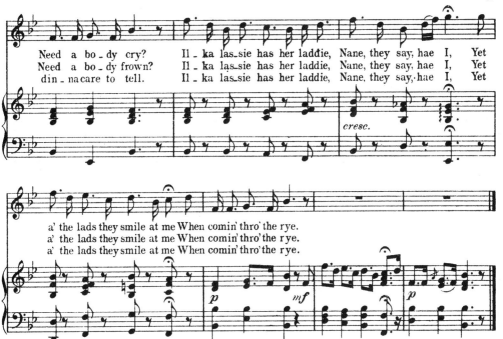

Auld Robin Gray.

LADY ANN LINDSAY.

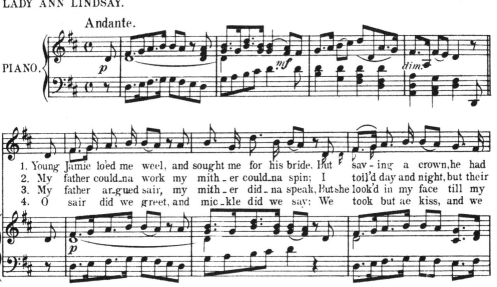

12

naething else be-side; To make the crown a pound my Ja_mie gaed to sea, And the
bread I could_na win; Auld Rob maintain'd them baith,and, wi'tears in his e'e, Said,
heart was like to break They gied him my hand,tho'my heart was at the sea, And
tore our_selves a_way. I wish that I were dead, but I'm no like to dee: Oh why

crown and the pound were baith for........ me." He
"Jen_ny, for their sakes,will ye no' mar_ry me?" My
auld Ro_bin Gray is..... gude_man to me. I
do I live to say,... O wae's...... me! I

p

had_na been gane a........ week but on_ly twa, When my
heart it said Na! for I look'd for Ja_mie back; But the
had_na been a wife, a week but on_ly four, When
gang like a ghaist, and I care_na to spin; I........

con dolore

fath_er brake his arm, and our cow was stown a_wa'; My
wind it blew high,and the ship it was a wrack; The
mourn_fu' as I sat on the stane at the door, I
dare_na think o' Jamie, for.... that wad be a sin. But

cresc. *mf*

mither she fell sick, and my Ja _ mie at the sea, And auld Ro_bin Gray cam' a
ship it was a wrack! why did _ na Jen _ ny dee? Oh why do I live to say,...
saw my Ja_mie's ghaist I could _ na think it he, Till he said, I'm come hame, my
I will do my best a gude wife aye to be, For auld Ro_bin Gray is a

court _ ing me.
O wae's me!"
love to mar _ ry thee!"
kind man to me.

Mary of Argyle.

Words by
JEFFERYS.

Music by
S. NELSON.

Andantino.

PIANO.

1. I have heard the ma_vis sing_ing His love song to the morn; I have
2. Tho' thy voice may lose its sweet_ness And thine eye its bright_ness too; Tho' thy

seen the dew drop clinging To the rose just new_ly born: But a sweet_er song has
step may lack its fleetness, And thy hair its sun_ny hue: Still to me wilt thou be

cheer'd me, At the ev'_ning's gen_tle close; And I've seen an eye still brighter, Than the
dear_er, Than all the world shall own; I have loved thee for thy beau_ty. But

dew-drop on the rose; 'Twas thy voice, my gen_tle Mary, And thine artless, winning smile, That
not for that a lone; I have sought thy heart, dear Mary, And its goodness was the wile, That h's

made this world an E_den, Bonnie Mary of Ar_gyle.
made thee mine for e_ver, Bonnie Mary of Ar_gyle.

Cam' ye by Athole.

Words by
JAMES HOGG.

Music by
NEIL GOW. Junr.

1. Cam' ye by Athole, lad wi' the phil _ a _ beg. Down by the Tummel, or banks o' the Gar _ ry? Saw ye the lads wi' their bon_nets and white cock_ades, Leav _ ing their moun _ tains to fol _ low Prince Char _ lie.
2. I ha'e but ae son, my gal _ lant young Don _ ald, But if I had ten they should fol _ low Glen _ gar _ ry. Health to McDon _ ald, and gal_lant Clan - Ron _ ald, For these are the men that will die for their Char _ lie.
3. I'll to Loc_hiel and Ap _ pin, and kneel to them; Down by Lord Mur_ray and Roy o' Kil _ dar _ lie. Brave Mac_kin_tosh he shall fly to the field wi' them, They are the lads I can trust wi' my Char _ lie.
4. Down thro' the Low _ lands, down wi' the Whig_a_more, Loy _ al true High_land _ers, down wi' them rare _ ly. Ron _ ald and Don _ ald drive on wi' the braid clay_more, O _ ver the necks o' the foes o' Prince Char _ lie.

Fol-low thee, fol-low thee, wha wad-na fol-low thee?

Lang hast thou lo'ed and trust-ed us fair-ly; Char-liè, Char-liè,

wha wad-na fol-low thee? King o' the Hie-lan' hearts,

bon-nie Prince Char-lie.

Within a mile o' Edinburgh town.

T. D'URFEY.

1. 'Twas with_in a mile o' E_din_bu_rgh town, In the ro_sy time of the year, Sweet flow_ers bloom'd and the grass was down, And each shepherd woo'd his dear. Bon_nie Jock_ie blythe and gay, Kiss'd young Jen_ny mak_ing, hay; The

2. Jock_ie was a wag that nev_er wad wed, Tho' long he had fol_low'd the lass; Con_tented she earn'd and ate her brown bread, And mer_ri_ly turn'd up the grass. Bon_nie Jock_ie blythe and free, Won her heart right mer_ri_ly, Yet

3. But when he vow'd he wad make her his bride, Tho' his flocks and herds were not few, She gied him her hand and a kiss be_side, And vow'd she'd for ever be true. Bon_nie Jock_ie blythe and free, Won her heart right mer_ri_ly At

las-sie blush'd, and frown_ing cried, Na, na, it win_na do; I can_na, can_na, win_na, win_na,
still she blush'd, and frown_ing cried, Na, na, it win_na do; I can_na, can_na, win_na, win_na,
kirk she no more frown_ing cried, Na, na, it win_na do; I can_na, can_na, win_na, win_na,

maun_na buck _ le to."
maun_na buck _ le to."
maun_na buck _ le to."

The Flowers of the Forest.

Words by
Mrs COCKBURN.

Larghetto con espressione.

VOICE.

1. I've seen the smil_ing Of
2. I've seen the morn_ing With

PIANO

for tune be _ guil _ ing, I've tast _ ed her plea_sures and felt her de_cay;
gold the hills a _ dorn _ ing, And loud tempests storm_ing be _ fore part_ing day.

Sweet was her bless_ing, And kind her ca_ress _ ing, But now they are fled they are
I've seen Tweed's silver streams, Shining in the sun_ny beams, Grow drumly and dark as they

fled far a_way; I've seen the for_est A_dorn_ed the fore_most, Wi'
roll'd on their way. Oh! fick_le for_tune! Why this cru_el sport_ing? Oh!

flow'rs o' the fair-est baith plea_sant and gay, Sae bonnie was their bloom_ing, Their
why still per_plex us, poor sons of a day? Thy frown can_na fear me, Thy

scent the air per_fum_ing, But now they are with_er'd and a' wede a_way.
smile can_na cheer me, Since the flow'rs o' the for_est are a' wede a_way.

Afton Water.

Words by
BURNS.

Music by
A. HUME.

1. Flow gent _ ly, sweet Af _ ton, a _ mang thy green braes, Flow gent _ ly I'll sing thee a
3. How loft _ y, sweet Af _ ton, thy neighbouring hills Far mark'd with the courses of
5. Thy crys _ tal stream, Af _ ton, how love _ ly it glides, And winds by the cot where my

song in thy praise; My Ma _ ry's a _ sleep by thy mur _ mur _ ing stream, Flow
clear wind _ ing rills, There dai _ ly I wan _ der as noon ris _ es high, My
Ma _ ry re _ sides; How wan _ ton thy wa _ ters her snow _ y feet lave, As

gent _ ly, sweet Af _ ton, dis _ turb not her dream.
flocks and my Ma _ ry's sweet cot in my eye.
gath _ 'ring sweet flowrets she stems thy clear wave.

2. Thou stock-dove whose e _ cho re _ sounds thro' the glen, Ye
4. How plea _ sant thy banks and green val _ leys be _ low, Where
6. Flow gen _ tly sweet Af _ ton, a _ mong thy green braes, Flow,

wild whist _ ling black _ birds in yon thorn _ y den, Thou.....................
wild in the wood _ lands the · prim _ ro _ ses blow, There.....................
gen _ tly, sweet riv _ er the theme of my lays: My.....................

green - crest _ ed lap _ wing, thy scream _ ing for - bear I
oft as mild eve _ ning, sweeps o _ ver the lea, The
Ma _ ry's a _ sleep by thy mur _ mur _ ing stream, Flow

charge you dis _ turb not my slum _ ber _ ing fair.
sweet - scent _ ed birk shades my Ma _ ry and me.
gen _ tly, sweet Af _ ton, dis _ turb not her dream.

Green grow the rashes, O.

Words by
BURNS.

1. There's nought but care on ev'_ry han', In ev'_ry hour that pas_ses, O! What
2. The warld_ly race may rich_es chase, An' rich_es still may fly them, O, An'
3. Gie me a can_tie hour at e'en, My arms a_bout my dear_ie, O: An'
4. And you sae douce, wha sneer at this, Ye're nought but sense_less ass_es, O! The

sig_ni_fies the life o' man, An' twere na' for the las_ses, O! Green grow the
tho' at last they catch them fast, Their hearts can ne'er en_joy them, O! Green grow the
warld_ly cares and warld_ly men May a' gae tap_sal_tee_rie, O! Green grow the
wis_est man the warld e'er saw, He dear_ly lo'ed the las_ses. O! Green grow the

rashes, O! green grow the rashes, O! The sweet_est hours that ere I spent Were
rashes, O! green grow the rashes, O! The sweet_est hours that ere I spent Were
rashes, O! green grow the rashes, O! The sweet_est hours that ere I spent Were
rashes. O! green grow the rashes, O! The sweet_est hours that ere I spent Were

spent a‿mang the las‿ses O!
spent a‿mang the las‿ses O!
spent a‿mang the las‿ses O!
spent a‿mang the las‿ses O!

5.
Auld Nature swears the lovely dears
Her noblest works she classes, O:
Her 'prentice han' she tried on man,
An' then she made the lasses, O.
Green grow the rashes, O! *etc.*

Scots, wha hae wi' Wallace bled!

Words by
BURNS.

PIANO.

Moderato.

1. Scots, wha. hae wi' Wal‿lace bled, Scots, wham Bruce has af‿ten led,
2. Wha would be a trait‿or knave? Wha would fill a coward's grave?
3. By op‿pres‿sion's woes an' pains, By your sons in ser‿vile chains,

24

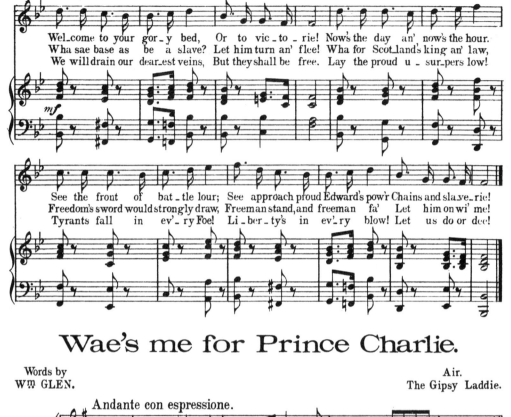

Wel_come to your gor_y bed, Or to vic_to_rie! Now's the day an' now's the hour.
Wha sae base as be a slave? Let him turn an' flee! Wha for Scot_land's king an' law,
We will drain our dear_est veins, But they shall be free. Lay the proud u_sur_pers low!

See the front of bat_tle lour; See approach proud Edward's pow'r Chains and sla_ve_rie!
Freedom's sword would strongly draw, Freeman stand, and freeman fa' Let him on wi' me!
Tyrants fall in ev'_ry Foe! Li_ber_ty's in ev'_ry blow! Let us do or dee!

Wae's me for Prince Charlie.

Words by
WM GLEN.

Air.
The Gipsy Laddie.

Andante con espressione.

PIANO.

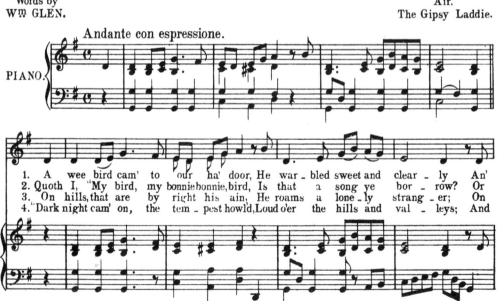

1. A wee bird cam' to our ha' door, He war_bled sweet and clear_ly An'
2. Quoth I, "My bird, my bonnie bonnie bird, Is that a song ye bor_row? Or
3. On hills, that are by right his ain, He roams a lone_ly strang_er; On
4. "Dark night cam' on, the tem_pest howl'd, Loud o'er the hills and val_leys; And

aye the o'er - come o' his sang Was wae's me for Prince Char _ lie.
is't some words ye've learnt by rote, Or a lilt o' dool and... sor _ row?
il _ ka hand he's press'd by want On il _ ka side by dan _ ger.
where was't that your Prince lay down, Wha's hame should been a pal _ ace?

O when I heard the bonnie, bonnie bird, The tears cam' drappin' rare _ ly; I
Oh! no, no, no!" the wee bird sang, I've flown since morning ear _ ly; But
Yes_treen I met him in the glen, My heart near bursted fair _ ly; For
He row'd him in a High_land plaid, Which cov _ er'd him but spare _ ly, And

took my bon _ net aff my head For weel I lo'ed Prince Char _ lie.
sic a day o' wind and rain! Oh! wae's me for Prince Char _ lie.
sad _ ly chang'd in _ deed was he Oh! wae's me for Prince Char _ lie.
slept be _ neath a bush o' broom Oh! wae's me for Prince Char _ lie.

5.
But noo the bird saw some red coats,
    And he shook his wings wi' anger:
"O, this is no a land for me,
    I'll tarry here no langer."
A while he hover'd on the wing,
    Ere he departed fairly;
But weel I mind the fareweel strain
    'Twas "Wae's me for Prince Charlie."

Bonnie Dundee.

Words by SIR WALTER SCOTT.

1. To the Lords of Con_ven_tion 'twas Cla_ver_house spoke: Ere the King's crown go down there are
2. Dun _ dee he is mount_ed, he rides up the street, The bells they ring back_ward, the
3. There are hills beyond Pentland, and lands be_yond Forth, Be there lords in the south, there are
4. Then a_wa' to the hills, to the lea, to the rocks, Ere I own a u_sur_per, I'll

crowns to be broke, Then each ca_va_lier who loves hon_our and me, Let him
drums they are beat, But the pro_vost(douce man) said,"Just e'en let it be, For the
chiefs in the north; There are brave Duin _ne_was_sels three thou_sand times three. Will cry,
crouch with the fox; And trem_ble, false whigs, in the midst o' your glee, Ye hae

fol _ low the bon _ nets of Bon _ nie Dun _ dee." Come
toun is weel rid o' that de'il o' Dun _ dee." Come
"Hey for the bon _ nets o' Bon _ nie Dun _ dee." Come
no seen the last o' my bon _ nets and me. Come

fill up my cup, come fill up my can, Come
fill up my cup, come fill up my can, Come
fill up my cup, come fill up my can, Come
fill up my cup, come fill up my can, Come

sad‿dle my hor‿ses, and call out my men; Un‿hook the west port, and
sad‿dle my hor‿ses, and call out my men; Un‿hook the west port, and
sad‿dle my hor‿ses, and call out my men; Un‿hook the west port, and
sad‿dle my hor‿ses, and call out my men; Un‿hook the west port, and

let us gae free, For its up wi' the bon‿nets of Bon‿nie Dun‿dee.
let us gae free, For its up wi' the bon‿nets of Bon‿nie Dun‿dee.
let us gae free, For its up wi' the bon‿nets of Bon‿nie Dun‿dee.
let us gae free, For its up wi' the bon‿nets of Bon‿nie Dun‿dee.

mf

Jock o' Hazeldean.

Words by Sir WALTER SCOTT.

1. "Why weep ye by the tide, la_dye? Why weep ye by the tide?...... I'll
2. "A chain of gold ye shall not lack, Nor braid to bind your hair,...... Nor
3. The kirk was deck'd at morn_ing tide The ta_pers glim_mer'd fair,...... The

wed ye to my young_est son, And ye shall be his bride;
met_tled hound, nor man_aged hawk, Nor pal_frey fresh and fair;
priest and bride_groom wait the bride, And dame and knight are there.

And ye shall be his bride la_dye, Sae come_ly to be seen," But
And you, the fair_est o' them a', Shall ride our for_est queen!" But
They sought her baith by bower and ha'_ The la_dye was not seen: She's

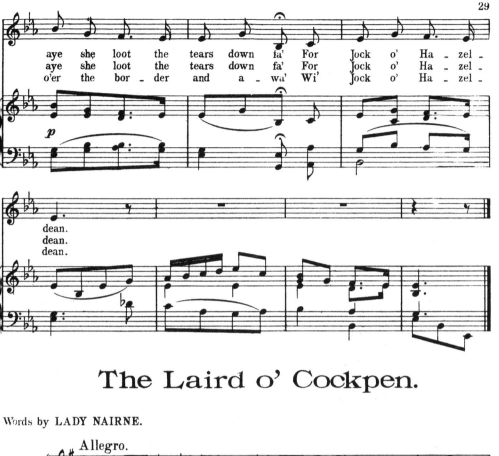

aye she loot the tears down fa' For Jock o' Ha _ zel _
aye she loot the tears down fa' For Jock o' Ha _ zel _
o'er the bor _ der and a _ wa' Wi' Jock o' Ha _ zel _

dean.
dean.
dean.

The Laird o' Cockpen.

Words by LADY NAIRNE.

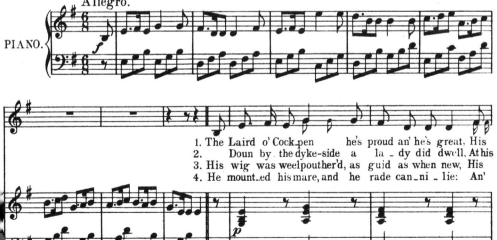

Allegro.

PIANO.

1. The Laird o' Cock_pen he's proud an' he's great, His
2.   Doun by . the dyke-side a la _ dy did dwell, At his
3. His wig was weel pouther'd, as guid as when new, His
4. He mount_ed his mare, and he rade can_ni _ lie: An'

30

mind is ta'en up wi' the things o' the state; He want_ed a wife his
ta_ble head he thocht she'd look well: M'_Cleish's ae doch_ter o'
waist_coat was white, his coat it was blue; He put on a ring, a
rapp'd at the yett o' Cla_vers'_ha' Lee. "Gae tell Mistress Jean to come

braw house to keep, But fa_vour wi' woo_in' was fash_ious to seek.
Cla_vers'_ha' Lee, A pen_ny_less lass, wi' a lang ped_i_gree.
sword and cock'd hat; And wha could re_fuse the Laird wi' a' that?
speed_i_ly ben; She's want_ed to speak wi' the Laird o' Cock_pen."

5.

Mistress Jean she was makin' the elder-flower wine
"What the deil brings the Laird here at sic a like time?"
She put aff her apron, an' on her silk goun,
Her mutch wi' red ribbon, an' gaed awa' doun.

6.

An' when she came ben, he bobbit fu' low;
An' what was his errand he soon let her know.
Amazed was the Laird when the lady said—"Na."
An' wi' a laigh curtsie she turned awa'.

7.

Dumbfounder'd was he— but nae sigh did he gi'e;
He mounted his mare, and he rade cannilie;
An' aften he thocht, as he gaed through the glen.
"She was daft to refuse the Laird o' Cockpen."

The Land o' the Leal.

Words by **LADY NAIRNE.**

1. I'm wear _ in' a _ wa', Jean, Like snaw wreaths in thaw, Jean, I'm wear _ in' a _
2. Ye aye, were leal and true, Jean, Your task's end _ ed noo, Jean, And I'll welcome
3. Then dry that tear _ fu' e'e, Jean, My soul langs to be free, Jean, And angels wait on

wa' To the land o' the leal. There's nae sor _ row there, Jean, There's nei - ther cauld nor
you To the land o' the leal. Our bon _ nie bairn's there, Jean, She was baith gude and
me To the land o' the leal. Now fare ye weel, my ain, Jean, This warld's care is

care, Jean, The day is aye fair, In the land o' the leal.
fair, Jean, And O we grudge her sair To the land o' the leal.
vain, Jean, We'll meet and aye be fain In the land o' the leal.

Ye Banks and Braes o' bonnie Doon

Words by BURNS.

1. Ye banks and braes o' bon_nie Doon, How can ye bloom sae fresh and fair? How
2. Oft hae I rov'd by bon_nie Doon, To see the rose and wood-bine twine. And

can ye chaunt, ye lit _ tle birds, And I sae wea _ ry fu' o' care? Ye'll
il _ ka bird sang o' its love And fond _ ly sae did I o' mine. Wi'

break my heart, ye warb _ ling bird, That wan _ tons thro' the flow _ 'ry thorn, Ye
light-some heart I pu'd a rose Fu' sweet up _ on its thorn _ y tree; And

mind me o' de_part_ed joys, De_part_ed ne_ver
my fause lov_er stole my rose, But ah! he left the

to re_turn.
thorn wi' me.

John Anderson, my Jo.

Words by BURNS.

Andante.

PIANO.

1. John An_der_son, my jo, John, When we were first ac_quent, Your
2. John An_der_son, my jo, John, We clamb the hill the_gith_er, And

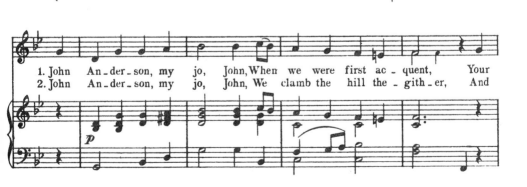

locks were like the ra _ ven, Your bon _ nie brow was brent, But
mony a can_tie day, John, We've had wi' ane a _ nith_er; Now

now your brow is bald, John, Your locks are like the snow, Yet
we maun tot_ter down, John, But hand in hand we'll go, And we'll

bless _ ings on your fros _ ty pow, John An _ der _ son, my jo.
sleep the_gith_er at the foot John An _ der _ son, my jo.

The Rowan Tree.

Words by LADY NAIRNE.

1. O rowan tree, O rowan tree, Thou'lt aye be dear to me En-
2. How fair wert thou in simmer time, wi' a' thy clus-ters white; How
3. We sat a-neath thy spreading shade, the bairn-ies round thee ran, They
4. Oh! there a-rose my fath-er's pray'r in ho-ly eve-ning's calm, How

twin'd thou art, wi' mo-ny ties o' hame and in-fan-cy
rich and gay thy au-tumn dress, wi' ber-ries red and bright,
pu'd thy bon-nie ber-ries red, and neck-la-ces they strang;
sweet was then my mith-er's voice, in the mar-tyrs' psalm!

cresc.

Thy leaves were aye the first o' spring, Thy flow'rs the sim-mer's pride; There
On thy fair stem were mo-ny names, which now nae mair I see, But
My mith-er, oh! I see her still, she smiled our sports to see, Wi'
Now a' are gane! we meet nae mair a-neath the row-an tree, But

was — na sic a bon — nie tree in a' the coun — try
they're en — gra — ven on my heart, for — got they ne'er can
lit — tle Jean — ie on her lap, and Ja — mie at her
hal — low'd thoughts a — round thee twine, o' hame and in — fan —

side. O row — an tree.
be. O row — an tree.
knee. O row — an tree.
cy. O row — an tree.

Come under my plaidie.

Words by HECTOR MACNEIL.

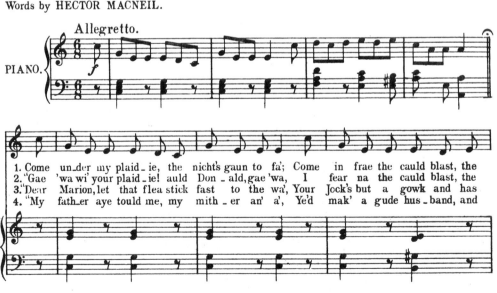

1. Come un — der my plaid — ie, the nicht's gaun to fa'; Come in frae the cauld blast, the
2. "Gae 'wa wi' your plaid — ie! auld Don — ald, gae 'wa, I fear na the cauld blast, the
3. "Dear Marion, let that flea stick fast to the wa', Your Jock's but a gowk and has
4. "My father aye tould me, my mith — er an' a', Ye'd mak' a gude hus — band, and

drift, and the snaw, Come un_der my plaid _ ie, and sit down be _ side me, There's
drift, nor the snaw, Gae 'wa wi' your plaid _ ie! I ll no sit be _ side ye, Ye
nae_thing a _ va; The hale o' his pack he has now on his · back;... He's
keep me aye braw; It's true I lo'e John _ nie, he's young and he's bon nie, But,

room in't, dear las _ sie; be _ lieve me, for twa. Come un _ der my plaid _ ie, and
might be, my gutcher, auld Don_ald, gae 'wa. I'm gaun to meet John _ nie, he's
thret _ ty, and I am but three_score and twa. Be frank now, and kind _ ly, I'll
waes me! I ken, he has nae_thing a _ va! I ha'e lit _ tle toch _ er, ye've

sit down be _ side me, I'll hap ye frae ev' _ ry cauld blast that can blaw Come
young and he's bon _ nie, He's been at Meg's bri _ dal, fu' trig and fu' blaw! Nane
busk ye aye fine _ ly, To kirk or to mar _ ket there'll few gang sae blaw; A
made a guid of _ fer; I'm noo mair than twen_ty, my time is but sma! Sae

un _ der my plaid _ ie and sit down be _ side me, There's
dan _ ces sae light _ ly sae grace _ fu', sae tight _ ly, His
bien house to bide in, a chaise for to ride in, An'
gie me your plaid _ ie, I'll creep in be _ side ye, I

room int dear las_sie be_lieve me, for twa.
cheeks like the new rose, his brows like the snaw."
flun_kies to tend ye as aft as ye ca!"
thocht ye'd been auld_er than three-score and twa!"

5. She crap in ayont him, beside the stane wa',
    Whar Johnnie was list'ning, and heard her tell a';
   The day was appointed!— his proud heart it dunted,
    And strack 'gainst his side as if burstin' in twa.
   He wander'd hame weary, the night it was dreary,
    And, thowless, he tint his gate 'mang the deep snaw;
   The howlett was screamin' while Johnnie cried, "Women
    Wad marry auld Nick, if he'd keep them aye braw."

6. O! the deil's in the lasses! they gang now sae braw,
    They tak' up wi' auld men o' fourscore and twa;
   The hale o' their marriage, is gowd and a carriage,
    Plain love is the cauldest blast now, that can blaw.
   Auld dotards, be wary! tak' tent wha you marry,
    Young wives, wi' their coaches, they'll whup and they'll ca',
   Till they meet wi' some Johnnie, that's youthfu' and bonnie,
    When, they'll wish that their auld men were dead and awa'.

Gloomy winter's noo awa'.

Words by TANNAHILL.

1. Gloom_y win_ter's noo a_wa', Saft the west_lin' breez_es blaw,
2. Tow'r_ing o'er the New_ton woods, Lav'_rocks fan the snaw-white clouds,

Mang the birks o' Stan _ ley shaw, The ma _ vis sings fu' cheer _ ie, O.
Sil _ ler saughs wi' down _ y buds, A _ dorn the banks sae brier _ y, O,

Sweet the crawflow'rs ear _ ly bell, Decks Glen _ if _ fer's dew _ y dell, Blooming like thy bonnie sel', My
Round the sil _ van fair _ y nooks, Feath'ry breckans fringe the rocks, 'Neath the brae the burnie jouks, And

young, and art _ less dearie, O. Come, my las _ sie let us stray O'er Glen _ kil _ loch's sunny brae,
il _ ka thing is cheerie, O; Trees may bud, and birds may sing, Flow'rs may bloom and verdure spring,

Blythe _ ly spend the gow _ den day, Midst joys that nev _ er wea _ ry, O.
Joy to me they can na' bring, Un _ less wi thee, my dear _ ie, O.

The Bonnie, Bonnie Banks o' Loch Lomon'.

1. By yon bon-nie banks and by you bon-nie braes, Where the sun shines bright on Loch Lo — mon' Where me and my true love were ev-er wont to gae On the bon-nie, bon-nie banks o' Loch Lo — mon'

2. 'Twas there that we part-ed in yon sha-dy glen, On the steep, steep side o' Ben Lo — mon' Where in pur-ple hue the..... hie-land hills we view, An' the moon com-in' oot in the gloam — in'.

3. The wee bird-ies sing, and the wild flow-ers spring An' in sun-shine the wa-ters are sleep — in' But the bro-ken heart, it...... kens nae sec-ond spring, Tho' the wae — fu' may cease frae their greet — in'.

DUET. *ad lib.*

O, you'll tak' the high road, and I'll tak' the low road, and

I'll be in Scot _ land a _ fore......... ye; But me and my true love will

nev _ er meet a _ gain On the bon_nie, bon_nie banks o' Loch

Lo _ _ _ mon!

Robin Adair.

1. What's this dull   town to me? Ro_bin's not near;   What was't I   wish'd to see?
2. What made th' as _ sem _ bly shine? Ro_bin A _ dair;   What made the ball so fine?
3. But now thou'rt cold to me Ro_bin A _ dair;   And I   no more shall see

What wish'd to   hear? Where's all the   joy and mirth, Made this town heav'n on earth,
Ro _ bin was   there. And when the   play was o'er What made my   heart so sore?
Ro _ bin A _ dair   Yet he I   loved so well, Still in   my   heart shall dwell,

Oh! they're all   fled   with thee, Ro _ bin A _ dair.
Oh! it   was   part _ ing with Ro _ bin A _ dair.
Oh! I   can   ne'er for _ get Ro _ bin A _ dair.

Of a' the airts the wind can blaw.

Words by BURNS.

1. Of a' the airts the wind can blaw, I dear-ly lo'e the west, For
2. Blaw, blaw ye wast-lin'winds, blaw saft, A-mang the leaf-y trees, Wi'

there the bon-nie las-sie lives, The las-sie I lo'e best; Let wildwoods grow and rivers flow, Wi'
gen-tle gale frae hill and dale, Bring hame the la-den bees; And bring the las-sie back to me, That's

mo-ny a hill be-tween, Baith day and night my fan-cy's flight, Is ev-er wi' my Jean. I
aye sae neat and clean, Ae smile o' her wad ban-ish care, Sae love-ly is my Jean. What

44

see her in the dew_y flow'rs, Sae love_ly fresh and fair; I
sighs and vows, a_mang the knowes, Hae pass'd a_tween us twa! How

hear her voice, in il_ka bird, Wi' mu_sic charm the air; There's
fain to meet, how wae to part, That day she gaed a_wa! The

not a bon_nie flow'r that springs, By foun_tain, shaw or green, There's
pow'rs a-bune can on_ly ken, To whom this heart is seen, That

not a bon_nie bird that sings, But minds me o' my Jean.
nane can be sae dear to me, As my sweet love_ly Jean.

My Nannie's awa'!

Words by BURNS.

1. Now in her green man _ tle, blythe Na _ ture ar _ rays, And lis _ tens the lamb _ kins that bleat o'er the braes. While birds war _ ble wel _ come in il _ ka green shaw; But to

2. The snow _ drop and prim _ rose our wood _ lands a _ dorn, And vi _ o _ lets bathe in the weet o' the morn; They pain my sad bo _ som, sae sweet _ ly they blaw! They

3. Thou lav' _ rock, that springs frae the dews o' the lawn, The shep _ herd to warn of the grey break _ in' dawn, And thou mel _ low ma _ vis, that hails the night _ fa'; Give

4. Come, au _ tumn, sae pen _ sive, in yel _ low and grey, And soothe me wi' ti _ dings o' Na _ ture's de _ cay; The dark, drear _ y win _ ter, and wild _ driv _ ing snaw. A _

me, it's de light less, my Nan nie's a wa', But to
mind me o' Nan nie and Nan nie's a wa', They
o ver for pi ty my Nan nie's a wa', Give
lane can de light me my Nan nie's a wa', A

me it's de light less, my Nan nie's a wa'.
mind me o' Nan nie and Nan nie's a wa'.
o ver for pi ty my Nan nie's a wa'.
lane can de light me my Nan nie's a wa'.

There's nae Luck about the House

Animato.

PIANO.

1. And are ye sure the news is true? And are ye sure he's weel? Is
2. Rise up, and mak' a clean fire-side, Put on the muc kle pot; Gie
3. Sae true his heart, sae smooth his speech, His breath like cal ler air! His
4. The cauld blasts o' the win ter wind, That thirl'd thro' my heart, They're

this a time to talk o' wark? Ye jades, fling by your wheel. Is this a time to
lit _ tle Kate her cot _ ton gown, And Jock his Sun _ day coat, And mak' their shoon as
ve _ ry foot has mu _ sic in't As he comes up the stair; And will I see his
a' blawn by; I hae him safe; 'Till death we'll ne _ ver part; But what puts part _ ing

think o' wark, When Co _ lin's at the door? Gi'e me my cloak, I'll to the quay, And
black as slaes, Their hose as white as snaw, It's a' to please my ain gudeman, For
face a _ gain? And will I hear him speak? I'm down-right diz _ zy wi' the thought, In
in my mind, It may be far a _ wa', The pre _ sent mo _ ment is our ain, The

CHORUS.

see him come a _ shore. For there's nae luck a _ bout the house, There's nae luck a _
he's been long a _ wa'. For there's nae luck a _ bout the house, There's nae luck a _
troth I'm like to greet. For there's nae luck a _ bout the house, There's nae luck a _
neist we ne _ ver saw! For there's nae luck a _ bout the house, There's nae luck a _

_ va'; There's lit _ tle plea _ sure in the house, When our gude _ man's a _ wa'.
_ va'; There's lit _ tle plea _ sure in the house, When our gude _ man's a _ wa'.
_ va'; There's lit _ tle plea _ sure in the house, When our gude _ man's a _ wa'.
_ va'; There's lit _ tle plea _ sure in the house, When our gude _ man's a _ wa'.

D.C.

My Love she's but a Lassie.

Words by BURNS.

PIANO.

Allegretto.

1. My love she's but a   las _ sie yet, My   love she's but a   las _ sie yet; We'l
2. Come draw a drap o' the   best o't yet; Come draw a drap o' the   best o't yet; Gae

let her stan' a   year or   twa, She'll   no be half sae   sau _ cy yet.
seek for plea _ sure where ye   will, But   here I nev _ er   miss'd it yet.

I   rue   the   day   I   sought   her,   O!   I
We're a'   dry   wi'   drink _ ing   o't;

rue the day I sought her, O! Wha gets her need _ na
We're a' dry wi' drink _ ing o't; The min _ is _ ter kiss'd the

rall.

say she's woo'd, But he may say he's bought her, O!
fid _ dler's wife, An' could _ na preach for think _ in' o't.

a tempo

D.C.

Roy's Wife o' Aldivalloch.

Words by Mrs GRANT of Carron.

Old Strathspey Melody,

Andantino.

VOICE.

PIANO.

1. Roy's wife o' Al _ di_val_loch,

Roy's wife o' Al_di_val_loch, Wat ye how she cheated me, As I cam' o'er the braes o' Balloch?

50

2. She vow'd, she swore she wad be mine, She said she lo'ed me best o' on - y But
3. For O! she was a can - ty quean, And weel could dance the High - land walloch; How
4. Her hair sae fair, her e'en sae clear, Her wee bit mou' sae sweet and bon - nie; To

O! the fic - kle faith - less quean, She's ta'en the carle an' left her John - nie.
hap - py I, had she been mine, Or I'd been Roy o' Al - di - val - loch.
me she ev - er will be dear, Tho' she's for ev - er left her John - nie.

CHORUS.

Roy's wife o' Al - di - val - loch, Roy's wife o' Al - di - val - loch,

p

Wat ye how she cheat - ed me, As I cam' o'er the braes o' Bal - loch?

Wandering Willie.

Words by BURNS.

1. Here a wa', there a wa', wan - der-ing Wil-lie, Here a wa', there a wa',
2. Win - ter winds blew loud and cauld at our parting; Fears for my Wil - lie brought
3. Rest ye wild storms, in the caves of your slumbers: How your dread howl-ing a
   oh if he's faith-less, and minds na his Nan-nie, Flow still be - tween us thou

haud a wa' hame, Come to my bo - som, my ain on - ly.... dear - ie
tears to my e'e; Wel-come, now sim-mer, and wel come my.. Wil - lie, The
lov - er a - larms! Wau-ken, ye breez-es! row gent - ly, ye.... bil-lows! And
wide roaring main! May I ne-ver see..... it, may I never trow it, But,

Tell me thou bring'st me my Wil - lie the same.
sim-mer to na - ture and Wil - lie to me.
waft my dear lad - die ance mair to my arms.
dy - ing be - lieve that my Wil-lie's my ain.

The Scottish Blue Bells.

Words by C. D. SILLERY.

Music by GEORGE BARKER.

1. Let the proud In _ dian boast of his jes _ sa _ mine bowers, His
2. Sub _ lime are your hills when the young day is beam_ing, And

pastures of per _ fume, and rose cov_er'd dells: While hum_bly I sing of these
green are your groves with their cool crys_tal wells; And bright are your broad-swords like

wild lit_tle flowers, The blue bells of Scot_land the Scot_tish blue bells; Wave,
morn_ing dew gleam_ing, On blue bells of Scot_land on Scot_tish blue bells; A

shout in the cho rus for ev er and ev er The
shout in the cho rus for ev er and ev er The

blue bells of Scot_land, the Scot_tish blue bells.
blue bells of Scot_land, the Scot_tish blue bells.

There grows a Bonnie Brier Bush.

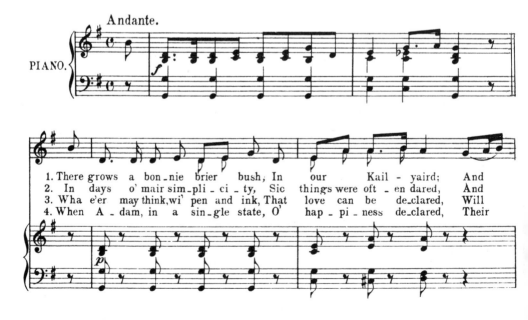

PIANO.

Andante.

1. There grows a bon_nie brier bush, In our Kail - yaird; And
2. In days o' mair sim_pli _ ci _ ty, Sic things were oft _ en dared, And
3. Wha e'er may think, wi' pen and ink, That love can be de_clared, Will
4. When A _ dam, in a sin_gle state, O' hap _ pi _ ness de_clared, Their

sweet are the blossoms o't, In our Kail-yaird. And in a - hint that bri - er bush, A
mony a maid's been woo'd and won, In her Kail-yaird. But noo they're sae par-tic - u - lar, Sae
find that pas - sion's by a pen, Maist woefully impair'd For me, I din-na like the love, That's
courtin' was be-gun, I trow. In their Kail-yaird. We'll fol - low then, the first o' men, Nor

bon-nie lass and lad, Are bu - sy, bu - sy court - in' In our Kail - yaird.
muc - kle on their guaird, That las - sies shake their heids at love, In our Kail - yaird.
writ-ten on a caird, I'd rath - er hae't by word o' mou' In our Kail - yaird.
be by fash-ion scared — As they be-gan we'll end the plan, In our Kail - yaird.

My heart is sair.

Words by BURNS.

1. My heart is sair, I daur - na tell, My heart is sair for some - bo-dy,
2. Ye pow'rs that smile on vir - tuous love, Oh! sweet - ly smile on some - bo-dy; Frae

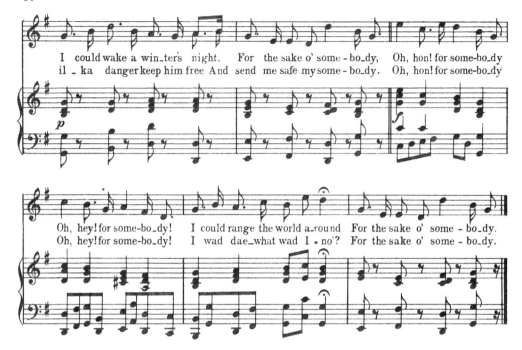

I could wake a win_ter's night, For the sake o' some-bo_dy, Oh, hon! for some-bo_dy,
il _ ka danger keep him free And send me safe my some-bo_dy. Oh, hon! for some-bo_dy

Oh, hey! for some-bo_dy! I could range the world a_round For the sake o' some - bo_dy.
Oh, hey! for some-bo_dy! I wad dae_what wad I _ no'? For the sake o' some - bo_dy.

The Birks of Aberfeldy.

Words by BURNS.

Allegretto.

PIANO.

CHORUS.

Bon_nie las_sie, will ye go, Will ye go, will ye go,

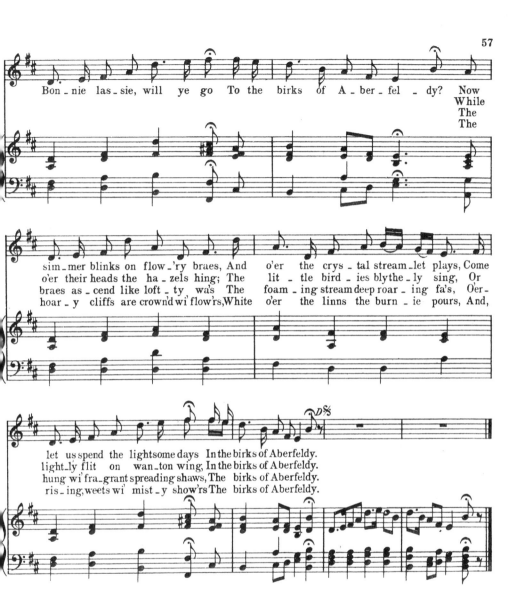

Bon - nie las - sie, will ye go To the birks of A - ber - fel - dy? Now
While
The
The

sim - mer blinks on flow - 'ry braes, And o'er the crys - tal stream - let plays, Come
o'er their heads the ha - zels hing; The lit - tle bird - ies blythe - ly sing, Or
braes as - cend like loft - ty wa's The foam - ing stream deep roar - ing fa's, O'er -
hoar - y cliffs are crown'd wi' flow'rs, White o'er the linns the burn - ie pours, And,

let us spend the lightsome days In the birks of Aberfeldy.
light - ly flit on wan - ton wing, In the birks of Aberfeldy.
hung wi' fra - grant spreading shaws, The birks of Aberfeldy.
ris - ing, weets wi' mist - y show'rs The birks of Aberfeldy.

Let fortune's gifts at random flee,
They ne'er shall draw a wish frae me,
Supremely blest wi' love and thee
In the birks of Aberfeldy.
Bonnie lassie, *etc.*

Mary Morison.

Words by BURNS.

Con espression.

PIANO.

1. O Ma ry, at thy win dow be, It is the wish'd the
2. Yes treen when to the trem bling string, The dance gaed thro' the
3. Oh Ma ry, canst thou wreck his peace, Who for thy sake would

tryst ed hour, Those smiles and glan ces let me see, That mak' the mis er's
light ed ha', To thee my fan cy took its wing, I sat, but neith er
glad ly dee? Or canst thou break that heart of his, Whase on ly fault is

cresc.

trea sure poor. How blithe ly wad I bide the stoure, A wea ry slave frae
heard nor saw. Tho' this was fair, and that was braw, And yon the toast of
lov ing thee? If love for love thou wilt na gie, At least be pi ty

sun to sun, Could I the rich re - ward se-cure, The love - ly Ma - ry
a' the town, I sigh'd, and said a - mang them a', Ye are na Ma - ry
to me shown; A thought un - gen - tle can - na be, The thought o' Ma - ry

Mo - ri - son.
Mo - ri - son.
Mo - ri - son.

"Ca' the Yowes to the Knowes."

Words by BURNS.

Moderato.

PIANO.

CHORUS.

Ca' the yowes to the knowes, Ca' them whaur' the hea - ther grows.

ca' them whaur' the bur‿nie rows, my bon‿nie dear‿ie.

1. Hark, the ma‿vis' ev'n‿in' sang Sound‿in' Clu‿den's woods a‿mang;
2. We'll gae down by Clu‿den side Thro' the ha‿zels spread‿ing wide
3. Yon‿der Clu‿den's si‿lent tow'rs, Where, at moon-shine mid‿night hours,
4. Ghaist nor bo‿gle shalt thou fear; Thou'rt to love and heav'n sae dear,

Then a fauld‿in' let us gang, My bon‿nie dear‿ie.
O'er the waves that sweet‿ly glide, To the moon sae clear‿ly.
O'er the dew‿y bend‿ing flow'rs Fair‿ies dance sae cheer‿ie.
Nocht o' ill may come thee near, My bon‿nie dear‿ie.

5.
Fair and lovely as thou art,
Thou hast stown my very heart;
I can die, but canna part,
  My bonnie dearie.

Flora Macdonald's Lament.

Words by HOGG.

Music by NEIL GOW Jun.ʳ

1. Far o - ver yon hills of the hea - ther sae.... green, And down by the cor - rie that sings to the sea, The bon - nie young Flo - ra sat sigh - ing her lane, The dew on her plaid, and the tear in her e'e.

2. The moor - cock that craws on the brow of Ben... Con - nal, He kens o' his bed in a sweet mos - sy hame, The ea - gle that soars on the cliffs of Clan - ron - ald, Un - awed and un - hunt - ed, his ey - rie can claim;

3. The tar - get is torn from the arm of the.... just,.... The hel - met is cleft on the brow of the brave, The clay - more for e - ver in dark - ness must rust: But red is the sword of the stranger and slave.

62

She look'd at a....boat, with the breez_es that swung, A _way on the wave, like a
The so _ lan can sleep on his shelve of the shore, The cor_mor_ant roost on his
The hoof of the horse, and the foot of the proud, Have trod o'er the plumes on the

bird of the main, And aye as it less_en'd she sigh'd and she sung, Fare_
rock of the sea; But oh! there is one whose hard fate I de _ plore, Nor
bon _ net of blue. Why slept the red bolt in the breast of the cloud, When

_weel to the lad I shall ne'er see a _ gain, Fare_weel to my he _ ro, the
house, ha', nor hame, in this coun_try has he,.... The con _ flict is past, and our
ty _ ran_ny rev_ell'd in blood of the true? Fare_weel, my young he _ ro! the

gal _ lant and young, Fare _ weel to the lad I shall ne'er see a _ gain.
name is no more: There's nought left but sor_row for Scot_land and me.
gal _ lant and good, The crown of thy fa-thers is torn from thy brow.

Bonnie Wee Thing.

Words by BURNS.

1. Bon_nie wee thing, can_nie wee thing, Lovely wee thing, wert thou mine, I would wear thee

in my bo_som, Lest my jew_el I should tine.
2. Wist_ful_ly I look and lan_guish
3. Wit and grace and love and beau_ty

In that bon_nie face o' thine; And my heart it stounds wi' anguish, Lest my wee thing be na mine.
In one star_ry clus_ter shine, To a_dore thee is my du_ty, Goddess o' this soul o' mine.

A Man's a Man for a' That.

Words by BURNS.

Allegretto.

PIANO.

mf

mp

1. Is there for hon_est pov_er_ty, That hangs his head, an' a' that? The
2. Ye see yon bir_kie ca'd a lord, Wha struts, and stares, and a' that, Tho'
3. A king can mak' a belt_ed knight, A mar_quis, duke, and a' that; But an
4. Then let us pray that come it may, As come it will, for a' that, That

cow_ard slave, we pass him by, We daur be puir for a' that. For
hun_dreds wor_ship at his word, He's but a coof for a' that. For
hon_est man's a_boon his micht, Gude faith, he maun_na fa' that! For
sense and worth, o'er a' the earth, May bear the gree, and a' that. For

a'....... that, and a'....... that, Our toils ob_scure, and a' that; The
a'....... that, and a'....... that, His rib_bon, star and a' that, The
a'....... that, and a'....... that, Their dig_ni_ties and a' that, The
a'....... that, and a'....... that, Its com_in' yet, for a' that, When

rank is but the gui _ nea's stamp, The man's the gowd for
man o' in _ de _ pen _ dent mind, He looks and laughs at
pith o' sense, and pride o' worth, Are high _ er ranks than
man to man the warld o'er, Shall brith _ ers be for

a' that.
a' that.
a' that.
a' that.

Oh! Whistle and I'll Come to You.

Words by BURNS.

With spirit.

PIANO.

Oh! whis_tle, and I'll come to you, my lad; Oh! whis_tle, and I'll come

to you, my lad: Tho' fa_ther and mi_ther and a' should gae mad, Oh!

whis_tle and I'll come to you, my lad.

1. But war_i_ly tent when ye
2. At kirk, or at mar_ket, when-
3. Aye vow and pro_test that ye

come to court me, And come na un_less the back _
e'er ye meet me, Gang by me as tho' that ye
care na for me, And whiles ye may light_ly my

yett be a_jee; Syne up the back stile, and let nae_bo_dy see, And
card na a flie; But steal me a blink o' your bon_nie black e'e, Yet
beau_ty a wee; But court na a_ni_ther, tho' jo_kin' ye be, For

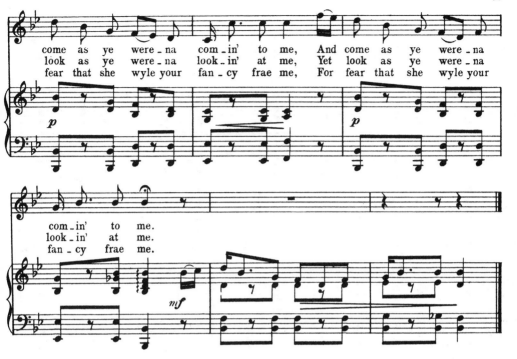

come as ye were _ na com _ in' to me, And come as ye were _ na
look as ye were _ na look _ in' at me, Yet look as ye were _ na
fear that she wyle your fan _ cy frae me, For fear that she wyle your

com _ in' to me.
look _ in' at me.
fan _ cy frae me.

Kate Dalrymple.

Words by WILLIAM WATT.

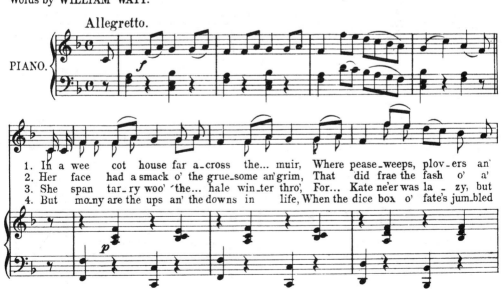

Allegretto.

PIANO.

1. In a wee cot house far a_cross the... muir, Where pease_weeps, plov_ers an'
2. Her face had a smack o' the grue_some an'grim, That did frae the fash o' a'
3. She span tar_ry woo' 'the... hale win_ter thro', For... Kate ne'er was la _ zy, but
4. But ma_ny are the ups an' the downs in life, When the dice box o' fate's jum_bled

whaups cry drear_y, There liv'd an' auld maid for mo_ny lang years, Wha
woo_ers de_fend her; Her lang Ro_man nose near_ly met wi' her chin, That
eid_ent and thrift_y; She wrocht 'mang the peats, coil'd the hay, shore the corn, An' sup_
a' tap_sal_tee_rie, Sae Kate fell... heir_ess to a rich frien's es_tate, An' nae

ne'er a woo_er did e'er ca'.....dear_ie. A lane__ly lass was...
brang folk in mind o' the auld witch o' En_dor. A wig_gle in her walk had...
_port_ed her sel' by her ain hard shift aye, But ne'er a lov_er came to.....
lan_ger for wooers had she cause to wear_y, The Laird cam' a-woo_in' soon o'

Kate Dal_rym_ple, A thrift__y quean was... Kate Dal_rym_ple; Nae
Kate Dal_rym_ple, A sni_vel in her talk... had... Kate Dal_rym_ple; An'
Kate Dal_rym_ple, For beau_ty an' toch_er want_ed Kate Dal_rym_ple; Un_
Kate Dal_rym_ple, The Law_yer, scrap_in', bow_in', fan oot Kate Dal_rym_ple; Owre

mu__sic, ex_cept__in' The clear burn_ie's wim_ple, Was
mo_ny a cor_ne__lian an cairn_gorm pim_ple, Did
_heed_ed was the quean, baith by gen_tle and sim_ple, A
ilk woo_ers face was seen love's smil_in'...... dim_ple, Sae

heard   round   the dwell _ in'   o'   Kate Dal_rym_ple.
blaze   on   the dun   face o'   Kate Dal_rym_ple.
blank   in ex _ is_tence seem'd puir Kate Dal_rym_ple.
noo   she's   nae mair, Kate, but Miss Dal_rym_ple.

5

She often times thocht when she dwelt by hersel',
She could wed Willie Speedyspool, the sarkin' weaver;
An' noo unto Will she the secret did tell
Wha for love or for interest did kindly receive her.
He flung by his beddles soon for Kate Dalrymple,
He brent a' his treddles doon for Kate Dalrymple;
Tho' his richt e'e doth skellie an' his left leg doth limp ill,
He's won the heart an' got the hand o' Kate Dalrymple.

The Hundred Pipers.

Words by LADY NAIRNE.

Allegretto.

PIANO.

1. Wi' a   hun _ dred pip _ ers, an'   a',   an' a', Wi' a
2. Oh! oor sodg _ er lads look'd braw, look'd braw, Wi' their
3. O!..... wha is fore - most o'   a',   o' a'! O!
4. The... Esk was swol _ len, sae red and sae deep, But

70

Car - lisle ha', Wi' its yetts, and cas tles an' a', an' a'.
look'd fu' wae, And mith - ers grat when they march'd a - way,
cur - ly hair, While the pi - pers blaw wi' an un - co flare!
wa' a - wa', Frae the hun - dred pi - pers an' a' an' a',

Wi' a hun - dred pi - pers, an' a', an' a', Wi' a

hun - dred pi - pers, an' a', an' a', We'll up and gie them a

blaw, a blaw. Wi' a hun - dred pi - pers an' a', an' a'.

Kelvin Grove.

Words by LYLE.

1. Let us haste to Kel _ vin grove, bon _ nie las _ sie, O; Thro' its ma _ zes let us rove, bonnie las _ sie, O; Where the ro _ ses in their pride, Deck the bon _ nie din _ gle side, Where the
2. Let us wan _ der by the mill, bon _ nie las _ sie, O, To the cove be _ side the rill, bonnie las _ sie, O, Where the glens re _ bound the call, Of the roar _ ing wa _ ters' fall, Thro' the
3. O......... Kel _ vin banks are fair, bon _ nie las _ sie, O, When the sum_mer we are there, bonnie las _ sie, O, There the May - pink's crim_son plume, Throws a soft but sweet per _ fume Round the
4. Tho' I dare not call thee mine, bon _ nie las _ sie, O, As the smile of for _ tune's thine, bonnie las _ sie, O, Yet with for _ tune on my side, I could stay thy fa _ ther's pride, And.....

mid_night fair_ies glide, bon_nie las _ sie, O.
mountains'rock_y hall, bon_nie las _ sie, O.
yel _ low banks o' broom, bon_nie las _ sie, O.
win thee for my bride, bon_nie las _ sie, O.

5. But the frowns of fortune lour, bonnie lassie, O,
   On thy lover at this hour, bonnie lassie, O,
   Ere yon golden orb of day
   Wake the warblers on the spray,
   From this land I must away, bonnie lassie, O.

6. Then farewell to Kelvin grove, bonnie lassie, O,
   And adieu to all I love, bonnie lassie, O,
   To the river winding clear,
   To the fragrant scented brier,
   Even to thee of all most dear, bonnie lassie, O,

7. When upon a foreign shore, bonnie lassie, O,
   Should I fall midst battle's roar, bonnie lassie, O
   Then, Helen, should'st thou hear
   Of thy lover on his bier,
   To his memory shed a tear, bonnie lassie, O.

Jessie the flower o' Dunblane.

Words by TANNAHILL.

1. The sun has gane down o'er the lof _ ty Ben-Lo_mond, And
2. She's mod _ est as on _ y and blythe as she's bon_nie, For
3. How lost were my days till I met wi' my Jes _ sie! The

left the red clouds to pre _ side o'er the scene; While lane _ ly I stray in the
guile _ less sim _ pli _ ci _ ty marks her its ain; And far be the vil _ lain, di _
sports o' the ci _ ty seem'd fool _ ish and vain; I ne'er saw a nymph I would

calm sim _ mer gloam _ in', To muse on sweet Jes _ sie, the flow'r o' Dun _ blane.
vest _ ed of feel _ ing, Wha'd blight in its bloom the sweet flow'r o' Dun _ blane.
ca' my dear las _ sie, Till charm'd wi' sweet Jes _ sie, the flow'r o' Dun _ blane.

How sweet is the brier wi' its saft fauld _ ing blos _ som, And sweet is the birk wi' its
Sing on, thou sweet ma _ vis, thy hymn to the e'en _ in', Thou'rt dear to the ech _ oes of
Tho' mine were the sta _ tion of lof _ ti _ est gran _ deur, A _ midst its pro _ fu _ sion I'd

man _ tle o' green; But sweet _ er and fair _ er, and dear to this bos _ om, Is
Cal _ der _ wood glen; Sae dear to this bos _ om, sae art _ less and win _ ning, Is
lan _ guish in pain. And reck _ on as nae _ thing the height o' its splen _ dour, If

charm_ing young Jes_sie, the flow'r o' Dun_blane, Is charm_ing young Jes_sie Is
charm_ing young Jes_sie, the flow'r o' Dun_blane, Is charm_ing young Jes_sie Is
want _ ing sweet Jes_sie, the flow'r o' Dun_blane, If want _ ing sweet Jes_sie If

charm_ing young Jes _ sie, Is charm_ing young Jes_sie the flow'r o' Dun_blane.
charm_ing young Jes _ sie, Is charm_ing young Jes_sie the flow'r o' Dun_blane.
want _ ing sweet Jes _ sie, If want _ ing sweet Jes_sie the flow'r o' Dun_blane.

D.C.

Thou Bonnie Wood o' Craigielea.

Words by TANNAHILL. **Music by JAMES BARR.**

1. Thou bon _ nie wood o' Crai _ gie _ lea, Thou bon _ nie wood o' Crai _ gie _ lea, Near

Fine.

thee I've spent life's ear_ly day, And won my Ma_ry's heart in thee.

The broom, the brier, the birk_en bush, Bloom bon_nie o'er thy flow_ry lea; And
2. Far ben thy dark green plan_tin's shade, The cush_at croo_dles am'rous_ly; The
3. A_wa', ye thoughtless murd'ring gang, Wha tear the nest_lings ere they flee! They'll
4. When win_ter blaws in slee_ty show'rs, Frae aff the Nor_lan hills sae hie, He

a' the sweets that ane can wish, Frae na_ture's hand are strew'd on thee.
ma_vis down thy bught_ed glade, Gars ech_o ring frae ev'_ry tree.
sing you yet a can_ty sang, Then, O, in pi_ty, let them be!
light_ly skiffs thy bon_nie bow'r, As laith to harm a flow'r in thee.

D.S.

5.
Though fate should drag me south the line,
Or o'er the wide Atlantic sea,
The happy hours I'll ever min',
That I in youth hae spent in thee.
Thou bonnie wood, *etc.*

Macgregor's Gathering.

Words by Sir WALTER SCOTT.

Music by ALEXANDER LEE.

The moon's on the lake, and the mist's on the brae, And the clan has a name that is
depths of Loch Ka_trine the steed shall ca_reer, O'er the peak of Ben Lo_mond the

name-less by day. Our sig _ nal for fight, which from monarchs we drew, Must be
gal _ ley shall steer, And the rocks of Craig Roy _ ston like i _ ci _ cles melt, Ere our

heard but by night in our venge _ ful ha _ loo,
wrongs be for _ got, or our ven _ geance un _ felt.

Then

ha_loo, ha_loo, ha_loo, Gre_ga_lach. If they

rob us of name, and pur _ sue us with Bea_gles, Give their

con valor.

roofs to the flame, and their flesh to the Eag_les. Then ga _ ther, ga _ ther,

ga_ther, ga _ ther, ga _ ther, ga _ ther, While there's

leaves in the fo_rest, and foam on the riv_er, Mac_gre_gor, de_spite them, shall

f

flour_ish for ev _ er.

ff

Glen _ or _ chy's proud moun_tain, Col _

Fine.

churn and her tow _ ers, Glen _ strae and Glen _ ly _ on, no

long-er are ours; We're land-less, land-less, land-less, Gre-ga-lach,

land-less, land-less, land-less Through the

ad lib.   *a tempo*   D.S.

D.S.

The Boatie Rows.

Moderato.

PIANO.

1. O   weel   may   the   boat-ie   row,   And   bet-ter   may   she   speed;   And
2. I   cuist   my   line   in   Lar-go   Bay,   And   fish-es   I   caught   nine;   There's
3. O   weel   may   the   boat-ie   row,   That   fills   a   hea-vy   creel,   And
4. When   Ja-mie   vow'd   he   wad   be   mine,   And   won frae   me   my   heart;   O

weel may the boat_ie row, That wins the bair_nie's bread. The boat_ie rows, the
three to roast, and three to boil, And three to bait the line. The boat_ie rows, the
cleeds us a' frae head to foot, And buys our par_ritch meal. The boat_ie rows, the
muc_kle light_er grew my creel! He swore we'd nev_er part. The boat_ie rows, the

boat_ie rows, The boat_ie rows in_deed; And hap_py be the lot of a' That
boat_ie rows, The boat_ie rows in_deed; And hap_py be the lot of a' That
boat_ie rows, The boat_ie rows in_deed; And hap_py be the lot of a' That
boat_ie rows, The boat_ie rows fu' weel, And muckle light_er is the load When

wish the boat_ie speed.
wish the boat_ie speed.
wish the boat_ie speed.
love bears up the creel.

5.
My kertch I put upon my head,
    And dress'd mysel' fu' braw,
I trow my heart was douff and wae
    When Jamie gaed awa'
But weel may the boatie row,
    And lucky be her part;
And lightsome be the lassie's care,
    That yields an honest heart.

6.
When Sandy, Jock and Janetie,
    Are up, and gotten lear,
They'll help to gar the boatie row,
    And lighten a' our care.
The boatie rows, the boatie rows,
    The boatie rows fu' weel;
And lightsome be the heart that bears
    The murlain and the creel.

Corn Rigs.

Words by BURNS.

smà per _ sua _ sion she a _ greed To see me thro' the
kiss'd her owre and owre a _ gain A _ mang the rigs o'
aye shall bless that hap _ py night, A _ mang the rigs o'
hap _ py night was worth them a', A _ mang the rigs o'

bar _ ley, O. Corn rigs and bar _ ley rigs,
bar _ ley, O. Corn rigs and bar _ ley rigs,
bar _ ley, O. Corn rigs and bar _ ley rigs,
bar _ ley, O. Corn rigs and bar _ ley rigs,

Corn rigs are bon _ _ nie; I'll ne'er for _ get that
Corn rigs are bon _ _ nie; I'll ne'er for _ get that
Corn rigs are bon _ _ nie; I'll ne'er for _ get that
Corn rigs are bon _ _ nie; I'll ne'er for _ get that

hap _ py night, A _ mang the rigs wi' An _ nie, O!
hap _ py night, A _ mang the rigs wi' An _ nie, O!
hap _ py night, A _ mang the rigs wi' An _ nie, O!
hap _ py night, A _ mang the rigs wi' An _ nie, O!

O, Nannie wilt thou gang wi' Me.

Words by BISHOP PERCY.   Music by THOMAS CARTER.

1. O Nan‿nie wilt thou gang wi' me, Nor sigh to leave the flaunting town? Can
2. O Nan‿nie when thou'rt far a‿way, Wilt thou not cast a look be‿hind? Say,
3. O Nan‿nie can'st thou love so true, Thro' per‿ils keen wi' me to go? Or
4. And when at last thy love shall die, Wilt thou re‿ceive his part‿ing breath, Wilt

si‿lent glens have charms for thee, The low‿ly cot, and rus‿set gown? No
can'st thou face the parch‿ing ray, Nor shrink be‿fore the win‿try wind? O,
when thy swain mis‿hap shall rue, To share with him the pang of woe? And
thou re‿press each strug‿gling sigh, And cheer with smiles the bed of death? And

long‿er dress'd in silk‿en sheen, No long‿er deck'd with jew‿els rare, Say,
can that soft and gen‿tle mien, Se‿ver‿est hard-ships learn to bear, Nor
when in‿vad‿ing pains be‿fall, Wilt thou as‿sume the nur‿se's care, Nor,
wilt thou o'er his breath‿less clay, Strew flow'rs, and drop the ten‿der tear; Nor

When the kye comes hame.

JAMES HOGG.

woo a bon-nie las-sie when the kye comes hame.
bon-nie, bon-nie las-sie when the kye comes hame.
miss a bon-nie las-sie when the kye comes hame.
meet his bon-nie las-sie when the kye comes hame.
When the kye comes hame, when the

kye comes hame, 'Tween the gloam - in' and the mirk, When the

kye comes hame.

5.

Awa' wi' fame and fortune—what comfort can they gie?
And a' the arts that prey upon man's life and libertie!
Gie me the highest joy that the heart o' man can frame,
My bonnie, bonnie lassie when the kye comes hame.
When the kye comes hame, *etc.*

Will ye no' come back again?

Words by LADY NAIRNE.

Music by NEIL GOW, Junr.

Andante.

PIANO.

1. Bonnie Charlie's noo awa; Safely owre the friendly main;
2. Ye trusted in your Hielan'men, They trusted you dear Charlie! They
3. English bribes were a' in vain, Tho' puir, and puirer, we maun be;
4. We watch'd thee in the gloamin' hour, We watch'd thee in the mornin grey; Tho'

Mony a heart will break in twa, Should he ne'er come back again.
kent your hiding in the glen, Death or exile braving.
Siller canna buy the heart, That beats aye for thine and thee.
thirty thousand pound they gie, Oh there is nane that wad betray!

CHORUS.

Will ye no' come back again. Will ye no' come back again? Better lo'ed ye

cresc.

mf

can_na be, Will ye no' come back a gain?

5

Sweet the laverock's note and lang,
Liltin' wildly up the glen;
But aye to me he sings ae sang,
Will ye no' come back again?
Will ye no' come, *etc.*

The Auld House.

Words by **LADY NAIRNE.**

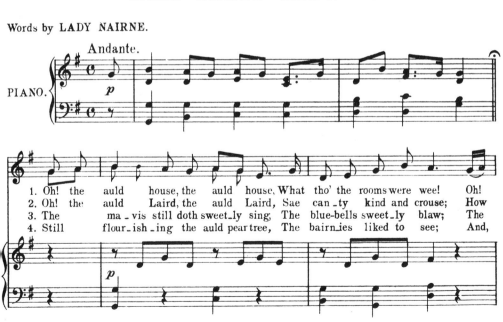

1. Oh! the auld house, the auld house, What tho' the rooms were wee! Oh!
2. Oh! the auld Laird, the auld Laird, Sae can_ty kind and crouse; How
3. The ma _ vis still doth sweet_ly sing, The blue-bells sweet_ly blaw; The
4. Still flour_ish_ing the auld pear tree, The bairn_ies liked to see; And,

kind   hearts were dwell _ ing there,   And bairn _ ies fu' o' glee;   The
mo _ ny did he wel _ come, to,   His ain wee dear, auld hoose!   And the
bon _ nie Earn's clear wind _ ing still,   But the auld house is a _ wa',   The
oh! how af _ ten did they speir,   When ripe they a' wad be?   The

wild - rose and the jes _ a _ mine, Still, hang up _ on the wa',   How
led _ dy too, sae gen _ _ ty,   There shel _ ter'd Scot _ land's heir,   And
auld house, the auld house, De _ sert _ ed tho' ye be,   There
voic _ es sweet, the wee bit feet, Aye rin _ nin' here and there;   The

mo _ ny cher _ ish'd mem _ o _ ries, Do they, sweet flow'rs, re _ ca'!
clipt a lock wi' her ain hand, Frae his lang yel _ low hair.
ne'er can be a new house, Will seem sae fair to me.
mer _ ry shout _ oh! whiles we greet, To think we'll hear nae mair.

p

5.	6.
For they are a' wide scatter'd noo!	The setting sun, the setting sun!
Some to the Indies gane;	How glorious it gaed doun!
And ane alas! to her lang hame;	The cloudy splendour rais'd our hearts
Not here we'll meet again _	To cloudless skies aboon!
The kirkyard, the kirkyard	The auld dial, the auld dial!
Wi' flowers o' every hue;	It told how time did pass;
Is sheltered by the holly's shade	The wintry winds ha'e dang it doun,
An' the dark sombre yew.	Now hid 'mang weeds and grass.

O, Willie Brew'd a Peck o' Maut.

Words by BURNS.

1. O, Wil_lie brew'd a peck o' maut, And Rob and Al_lan cam' to pree; Three
2. Here are we met, three mer_ry boys Three mer_ry boys I trow are we; And
3. It is the moon-I ken her horn—That's blink_ing in the lift sae hie; She
4. Wha first shall rise to gang a _ wa, A cuck_old, cow_ard loon is he! Wha

blyth _ er hearts that lee_lang night,Ye wad_na find in Chris_ten_die.
mony a nicht we've mer_ry been, And mo_ny mae we hope to be. We
shines sae bricht to wile us hame,But by my sooth she'll wait a wee.
last be_side his chair shall fa, He is the king a _ mang us three!

are na fou, we're no that fou, But just a drap_pie in our e'e; The

cock may craw, the day may daw, But aye we'll taste the bar _ ley bree.

Oh! Why Left I My Hame.

Words by R. GILFILLAN.

Andante moderato.

PIANO.

1. Oh,.... why left I my hame, Why.... did I cross the deep, Oh,.....
2. The... palm tree wav_eth high, And.... fair the myr_tle springs, And....
3. Oh!.... here no Sab_bath bell, A _ wakes the Sab_bath morn, Nor.....
4. There's a hope for ev'_ry woe, And a balm for ev'_ry pain, But the

why left I the land, Where my fore - fa - thers sleep? I.......
to the In - dian maid, The bul - bul sweet - ly sings, But I
song of reap - ers heard, A - mang the yel - low corn, For the
first joy of our heart, Comes nev - er back a - gain; There's a

rall.

sigh for Sco - tia's shore, And I gaze a - cross the
din - na see the broom, Wi' its tas - sels on the
ty - rant's voice is here, And the wail of sla - ver -
track up - on the deep, And a path a - cross the

colla voce

p espress.

sea, But I can - na get a blink, O'..... my
lea, Nor........ hear the lin - tie's sang, O'..... my
y, But the sun of free - dom shines, In.... my
sea, But the wea - ry ne'er re - turn, To.... their

p

rall.

ain.... coun - trie.
ain.... coun - trie.
ain.... coun - trie.
ain.... coun - trie.

mf

Gae bring to me a Pint o' Wine.

Words by BURNS.

1. Gae bring to me a pint o' wine, and fill it in......... a sil _ ver
2. The trum_pets sound, the ban_ners fly, The glit _ 'ring spears are rank_ed

tas _ sie, That I may drink be _ fore I go, A ser_vice
rea _ dy, The shouts of war are heard a _ far, The bat _ tle

to......... my bon _ nie las_sie. The boat rocks at......... the pier O'
clo _ ses deep and blood_y! It's not the roar......... o' sea or

Leith, Fu' loud the wind blaws frae the fer_ry, The ship rides
shore, Wad mak' me lan _ ger wish to tar_ry, Nor shouts o'

by.......... the Ber_wick Law, And I maun leave.... my bon_nie Ma_ry.
war........ that's heard a _ far, It's leav_ing thee..... my bon_nie Ma_ry.

CHORUS.

Gae bring to me a pint o' wine, And fill it in......... a sil _ver

tas_sie, That I may drink be_fore I go, A ser_vice to...... my bon_nie las_sie.

D. C.

The Lea Rig.

Words by BURNS.

1. When o'er the hill the east — ern star, Tells bught _ in time is near, my jo, And ow _ sen frae the fur _ row'd field, Re turn sae dowf and wear _ ie, O; Down by the burn, where scent _ ed birks, Wi'

2. In....... mirk _ est glen, at mid _ night hour, I'd rove, and ne'er be eer _ ie, O, If.... thro' that glen I gaed to thee, My ain....... kind....... dear _ ie, O. Al - tho' the night were ne'er sae wild, And

3. The.... hunt _ er lo'es the morn _ ing sun, To rouse the moun _ tain deer, my jo; At... noon the fish _ er seeks the glen, A long the burn to... steer, my jo; Gie me the hour o' gloaming grey, It

dew are hang_ing clear, my jo, I'll... meet thee on the lea........ rig, My
I..... were ne'er sae wear_ie, O, I'd... meet thee on the lea........ rig, My
maks my heart sae cheer_y, O, To... meet thee on the lea........ rig, My

ain....... kind.......... dear _ ie, O.
ain....... kind.......... dear _ ie, O.
ain....... kind.......... dear _ ie, O.

Scotland Yet.

Words by H. S. RIDDLE.

Music by P. Mc LEOD.

Con spirito.

PIANO.

1. Gae bring my guid auld harp ance mair, Gae bring it free and fast, For
2. The heath waves wild up_on the hills, And foam_ing frae the fells, Her
3. The this_tle wags up_on the fields, Where Wal_lace bore his blade, That
4. They tell o' lands with bright_er skies, Where free_dom's voice ne'er rang: Gie

I maun sing an i - ther sang, Ere a' my glee be
foun - tains sing of free - dom still, As they dance down the
gave her foe - men's dear - est bluid, To dye her auld grey
me the hills where Os - sian dwelt, And Coi - la's min - strel

past. And trow ye, as I sing, my lads, The
dells. And weel I lo'e the land, my lads, That's
plaid; And look - ing to the lift, my lads, He
sang! For I've nae skill o' lands, my lads, That

bur - den o't shall be, Auld Scot - land's howes and
gird - ed by the sea; Then Scot - land's vales, and
sang this dough - ty glee: Auld Scot - land's right, and
ken na to be free: Then Scot - land's right, and

Scot - land's knowes, And Scot - land's hills for me! I'll
Scot - land's dales, And Scot - land's hills for me! I'll
Scot - land's might, And Scot - land's hills for me! Then
Scot - land's might, And Scot - land's hills for me! We'll

rall. ad lib.

drink a cup to Scot - land yet, Wi' a' the hon - ours three!
drink a cup to Scot - land yet, Wi' a' the hon - ours three!
drink a cup to Scot - land yet, Wi' a' the hon - ours three!
drink a cup to Scot - land yet, Wi' a' the hon - ours three!

mf *colla voce* *f*

O Wert Thou in the Cauld Blast.

Words by BURNS.

Music by MENDELSSOHN.

Andante.

PIANO.

1. O wert thou in the cauld blast, On yon - der lea, On yon - der lea, My
2. Or were I in the wild - est waste, Sae bleak and bare, Sae bleak and bare, The

plai _ die to the an _ gry airt,.............. I'd shel _ ter thee, I'd
des _ ert were a pa _ ra _ dise,.............. If thou wert there If

shel _ ter thee; Or, did mis _ for _ tune's bit _ ter storms, A _
thou wert there. Or were I mon _ arch of the globe, With

_ round thee blaw, A round thee blaw, Thy bield should be my
thee to reign, With thee to reign, The bright _ est jew _ el

bo _ som, To share it a', To share it a'.
in my crown, Would be my Queen, Would be my Queen.

D. C.

Castles in the Air.

Words by JAMES BALLANTINE.

Andante.

PIANO.

1. The bon-nie, bon-nie bairn wha sits pok-in' in the ase,
2. He sees muc-kle cas-tles tow'r-in' to the moon! He
3. Sic a nicht in win-ter may weel.... mak' him cauld; His

Glow'r-in' in the fire wi' his wee round face; Laugh-in' at the fuff-in' lowe,
sees lit-tle sodgers pu-in' them a'... doun! Worlds whomb-lin' up and doun,
chin up-on his buffy hand will soon mak'him auld; His brow is brent sae braid Oh!...

what sees he there? Ha! the young dreamer's bigg-in' cas-tles in the air. His
blaz-in' wi' a flare, See how he loups as they glim-mer in the air. For
pray that dad-dy Care Would let the wean a-lane wi' his cas-tles in the air! He'll

wee chub_by face, and his tou _ zie cur _ ly pow, Are
a' sae sage he looks, what can the lad _ die ken? He's
glo _ wer at the fire! and he'll keek...... at the licht, But

laugh _ in' and nod _ din' to the danc _ in lowe; He'll...
think _ in' up_on nae _ thing, like mo _ ny might _ y men; A......
mo _ ny spark _ lin' stars are swal _ low'd up by nicht;

brown his ro _ sy cheeks and..... singe his sun _ ny hair,
wee thing makes us think, a....... sma' thing makes us stare, **There are**
Auld _ er e'en than his are...... glam _ our'd by a glare,

Glowr _ in' at the imps.... wi' their cas _ tles in the air.
mair........ folk than him..... bigg _ in' cas _ tles in the air.
Hearts are bro _ ken; heads are turn'd wi' cas _ tles in the air.

D. C.

My ain fireside.

Words by HAMILTON.

1. O   I   hae   seen   great   anes and   sat   in great   ha's,   'Mang
2. Ance   mair, heav'n be   praised! round my   ain   heartsome   in_gle, Wi' the
3. Nae   false _ hood   to   dread.... nae   mal _ ice   to   fear,   But....

lords and 'mang la _ dies a' cov _ er'd wi' braws; But a sight sae de _ light_ful I
frien's o' my youth I cor _ dial _ ly mingle; Nae forms to com _ pel me to
truth to de _ light me, and friend-ship to cheer; O' a' roads to hap _ pi _ ness

trow I ne'er spied, As the bon _ nie blythe blink o' my ain..... fire-side, My...
seem wae or glad, I may laugh when I'm mer _ ry, and sigh when I'm sad. My...
ev _ er were tried, There's nane half sae sure as ane's ain..... fire-side, My...

ain.... fire - side, my ain..... fire - side, O, sweet is the blink o' my
ain.... fire - side, my ain..... fire - side, O, sweet is the blink o' my
ain.... fire - side, my ain..... fire - side, O, sweet is the blink o' my

ain.... fire - side.
ain.... fire - side.
ain.... fire - side.

Highland Mary.

Words by BURNS.

PIANO.

Lento.

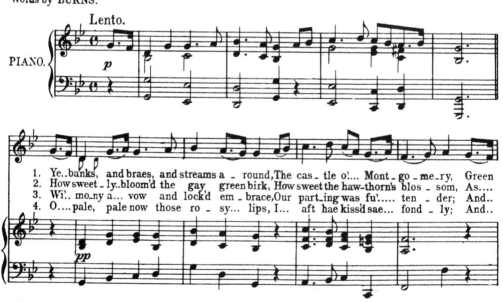

1. Ye..banks, and braes, and streams a _ round, The cas_ tle o'.... Mont_go_me_ry, Green
2. How sweet_ly..bloom'd the gay green birk, How sweet the haw-thorn's blos _ som, As....
3. Wi'.. mo_ny a... vow and lock'd em _ brace, Our part_ing was fu'..... ten _ der; And..
4. O....pale, pale now those ro_ sy... lips, I... aft hae kiss'd sae... fond _ ly; And..

be   your woods   and   fair   your flow'rs, Your   wa _ ters nev _ er.....
un _ der _ neath   their fra _ grant shade, I   clasp'd her to..... my...
pledg _ ing.... aft   to   meet   a _ gain, We   tore   our _ selves a _
closed for.... aye   the spark _ ling glance, That dwelt on   me sae...

drum _ lie!   There   sim _ mer first   un _ faulds her....robes, And
bo _ som! The.... gol _ den hours,   on   an _ gel....wings, Flew
sun _ der: But,...   oh! fell death's   un _ time _ ly   frost,   That
kind _ ly;   And   mould _ 'ring now   in   si _ lent dust,   The

there they lang _ est   tar _ ry, For there I took   the   last fare _ well, O'
o'er   me and my   dear _ ie; For dear to me   as   light and life, Was
nipt my flow'r sae   ear _ ly! Now green's the sod, and cauld's the clay, That
heart that lo'ed me   dear _ ly! But still within   my   bo _ som's core, Shall

my.... sweet High _ land Ma _ ry.
my.... sweet High _ land Ma _ ry.
wraps my... High _ land Ma _ ry.
live... my... High _ land Ma _ ry.

dim.

Lochnagar.

Words by LORD BYRON.

1. A - way, ye gay land - scapes, ye gar - den of ro - ses, In
2. Ah, there my young 'foot - steps, in in - fan - cy wan - der'd, My
3. Years have roll'd on, Loch - na - gar, since I left you!

you let the min - ions of lux - u - ry rove; Re - store me the rocks where the
cap was the bon - net, my cloak was the plaid; On chief - tians de - part - ed my
Years must e - lapse ere I see you a - gain; Tho' na - ture of ver - dure and

snow - flake re - pos - es, If still they are sa - cred to free - dom and love.
mem - o - ry pon - der'd, As dai - ly I stray'd thro' the pine cov - er'd glade. I
flow'rs, has bereft you, Yet still thou art dear - er than Al - bi - on's plain.

Yet   Cal - e - do - nia,.... dear   are   thy moun - tains,
sought   not   my home   till the   days   dy - ing glo - ry.....
Eng - land   thy beau - ties are   tame   and   do - mes - tic, To

Round their white sum-mits   tho' e - le - ments war,   Tho'   ca - ta - racts foam 'stead of
Gave   place   to the rays of the bright po-lar star,   For   fan - cy was cheer'd by tra-
one   who has roved on   the mountains a - far,   Oh!.... for the crags that are

smooth   flow - ing.. foun - tains,   I   sigh   for   the val - ley   of......
di - tion - al... sto - ry,   Dis - closed   by   the na - tives of......
wild...... and ma - jes - tic,   The   steep   frown - ing glo - ries of......

dark   Loch - na-gar.
dark   Loch - na-gar.
dark   Loch - na-gar.

Ilka Blade o' Grass.

Words by JAMES BALLANTINE.

Andante.

PIANO.

1. Con _ fide ye aye in Pro _ vi _ dence, for Pro _ vi _ dence is
2. Gin reft frae friends, or cross'd in love, as whiles nae doubt ye've
3. In lang, lang days o' sim _ mer, when the clear an' cloud _ less
4. So lest 'mid For _ tune's sun _ shine we should feel owre proud an'

kind, And bear ye, a' life's chan _ ges wi' a calm and tran _ quil
been, Grief lies deep hid _ den in your heart, or tears flow frae your
sky, Re _ fu _ ses ae wee drap o' rain to Na _ ture parch'd an'
hie, An' in our pride for _ get to wipe the tear frae poor tith's

mind, Tho' press'd and hemm'd on ev _ 'ry side, hae faith and ye'll win
een; Be lieve it for the best, an' trow there's gude in store for
dry, The ge _ nial night, wi' balm _ y breath, gars ver _ dure spring a-
e'e; Some wee dark cluds o' sor _ row come, we ken na whence or

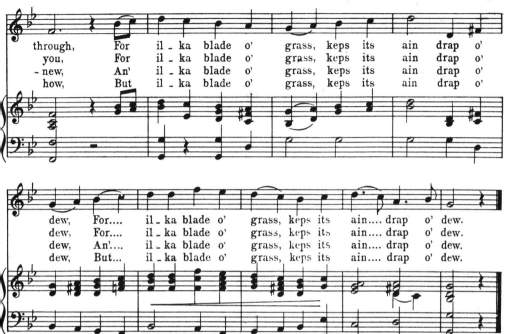

through,   For   il - ka blade o' grass, keps its ain drap o'
you,   For   il - ka blade o' grass, keps its ain drap o'
- new,   An'   il - ka blade o' grass, keps its ain drap o'
how,   But   il - ka blade o' grass, keps its ain drap o'

dew,   For....   il - ka blade o' grass, keps its ain.... drap o' dew.
dew,   For....   il - ka blade o' grass, keps its ain.... drap o' dew.
dew,   An'....   il - ka blade o' grass, keps its ain.... drap o' dew.
dew,   But...   il - ka blade o' grass, keps its ain.... drap o' dew.

D.C.

To Mary in Heaven.

Words by BURNS.

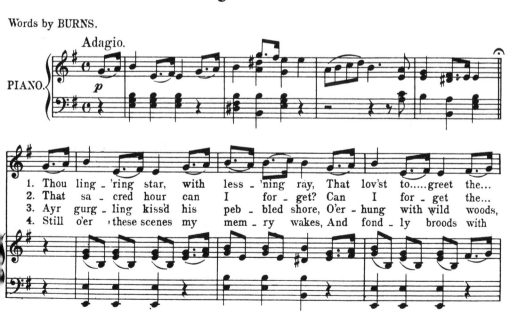

Adagio.

PIANO.

1. Thou ling - 'ring star, with less - 'ning ray, That lov'st to.....greet the...
2. That sa - cred hour can I for - get? Can I for - get the...
3. Ayr gurg - ling kiss'd his peb - bled shore, O'er - hung with wild woods,
4. Still o'er these scenes my mem - ry wakes, And fond - ly broods with

ear _ ly.... morn, A _ gain thou ush _ er'st in the..... day My...
hal _ low'd grove, Where by the wind _ ing, Ayr we..... met, To....
thick _'ning green; The frag _ rant birch the haw _ thorn hoar, Twin'd
mi _ ser care! Time but the im _ pres _ sion strong _ er...... makes, As...

Ma _ ry from my soul was.. torn. O...... Ma _ ry! dear de _
live one day of part _ ing... love? E _ ter _ ni _ ty.... will
am _ 'rous round the rap _ tur'd scene. The... flow'rs sprang wan _ ton
streams their chan _ nels deep _ er..... wear. My.... Ma _ ry, dear de _

_part _ ed.....shade! Where is thy place of.... bliss _ ful rest? See'st
not ef _ face, Those re _ cords dear of.... trans _ ports past; Thy...
to be.... prest, The birds sang love on... ev _ 'ry... spray, Till...
_part _ ed.... shade! Where is thy bliss _ ful... place of... rest? See'st

thou thy lov _ er low _ ly....laid? Hear'st thou the groans that rend... his breast?
im _ age at our last em _ brace, Ah! lit _ tle thought we 'twas... our last.
too, too soon, the glow _ ing west, Pro _ claim'd the speed of wing _ ed day.
thou thy lov _ er low _ ly....laid? Hear'st thou the groans that rend... his breast?

D. C

Auld Lang Syne.

Words by BURNS.

Moderato.

PIANO.

1. Should auld ac-quain-tance be for-got, And nev-er brought to min'? Should
2. We twa hae run a-bout the braes, And pu'd the gow-ans fine; But we've
3. We twa hae paid-l't in the burn, Frae morn-ing sun till dine; But
4. And there's a hand, my trust-y frien', And gie's a hand o' thine; And we'll

auld ac-quain-tance be for-got, And days o' lang... syne?
wan-der'd mo-ny a wea-ry foot, Sin' auld..... lang.... syne.
seas be-tween us braid hae roar'd, Sin' auld..... lang.... syne.
tak' a right gude wil-ly-waught, For auld..... lang.... syne.

For

auld lang..... syne, my dear, For auld lang..... syne, We'll

tak' a cup o' kind _ ness yet, For auld....... lang....... syne.

5.

And surely ye'll be your pint stoup
As surely I'll be mine!
And we'll tak' a cup o' kindness yet,
For auld lang syne.

Chorus.— For auld lang syne, my dear,
For auld lang syne,
We'll tak' a cup o' kindness yet,
For auld lang syne.

SO-AZT-860

SEP 1 - 2019

A small price to pay...

Thaddeus Blinn let the tent fl[ap]
fall and turned toward us. T[he]
expression on his face showed [he]
wasn't too happy about having so few [of]
us there. "Alas!" he said with a sigh. "S[o]
many people just cannot make themselve[s]
believe."

"I'm not really sure I believe you myself," said Rowena. "I read the sign and
came in because I was curious. What is it
you're selling, Mr. Blinn?"

"I'm selling wishes, child." Blinn spread
his hands as if it was the most obvious
thing in the world. "Anything you want—
anything you could possibly imagine—
can be yours!"

All of us on the bench looked at o[ne]
another, and Polly kind of giggled. I w[on-]
dered if Mr. Blinn was crazy in the head.

"I would love to get a wish," Row[ena]
said. "But it all sounds so . . . so incredi[ble."]

"I deal in the incredible," Blinn re[plied]
with a vast grin. "But before I go furt[her, I]
must have my fee. Fifty cents from e[ach of]
you, if you please."

The Wish Giver

Three Tales of Coven Tree

by Bill Brittain
drawings by Andrew Glass

HarperTrophy

A Division of HarperCollins*Publishers*

PROPERTY OF
PLACENTIA LIBRARY DISTRICT
411 EAST CHAPMAN AVENUE
PLACENTIA. CA 92870

The Wish Giver

Text copyright © 1983 by William Brittain

Illustrations copyright © 1983 by Andrew Glass

All rights reserved. No part of this book may be
used or reproduced in any manner whatsoever without
written permission except in the case of brief quotations
embodied in critical articles and reviews. Printed in
the United States of America. For information address
HarperCollins Children's Books, a division of
HarperCollins Publishers, 195 Broadway,
New York, N.Y. 10007

Library of Congress Cataloging in Publication Data
Brittain, Bill.
 The wish giver.

 Summary: When a strange little man comes to the
Coven Tree Church Social promising he can give people
exactly what they ask for, three young believers-in-
magic each make a wish come true in the most
unexpected way.
 [1. Wishes—Fiction. 2. Magic—Fiction] I. Glass,
Andrew, ill. II. Title.
PZ7.B78067Wi 1983   [Fic]   82-48264
ISBN 0-06-020686-1
ISBN 0-06-020687-X (lib. bdg.)
ISBN 0-06-440168-5 (pbk.)

First Harper Trophy edition, 1986.
18 19 20 BRR 60 59 58 57 56 55 54 53 52

36018057191470

For Jim and Sue—
who make me proud

The Tales

The Strange Little Man

Here in Coven Tree we're no strangers to magic. I'm not talking about the rabbit-from-a-hat or coin-up-the-sleeve variety, either. I mean *real* magic.

Witches have abounded in this part of New England since colonial days, when Cotton Mather held his witch trials in Salem to be rid of them. The very name of our village comes from the huge, twisted tree down at the crossroads where groups of witches—*covens*, they're called—used to meet. Imps and fiends and all the rest of Satan's spawn have appeared here from time to time, taking their pleasure from plaguing and frightening us poor mortals. Some folks even tell of seeing the Devil himself, walking about and looking for souls to claim when the mists hang low on the mountains.

Usually, though, these creatures of darkness can be recognized at once. Their appearance. The sounds that issue from them. Their manner of movement. The dismal swamps where they abide. All these bespeak their evil nature.

That's what was so odd about Thaddeus Blinn. There wasn't anything spooky or scary about him—at least nothing you could put your finger on. He seemed like just a funny little man who came to Coven Tree from out of nowhere with a strange tale about being able to give people exactly what they asked for. It wasn't until after the wishing started that . . .

But I'd best tell the story from front to back, the way it ought to be told. Polly and Rowena and Adam were each a part of what went on, to be sure. But it's myself who knows the whole thing.

Stew Meat's my name. I was christened Stewart Meade, but the nickname was hung on me as a boy, and it stuck. I own the Coven Tree General Store. The people for miles around shop here, and sooner or later everything they have to tell reaches my ears. So who better to relate the entire tale of Thaddeus Blinn and the awful trouble he brought to our peaceful little village?

The Coven Tree Church Social is always held the third Saturday in June on the church's big side lawn. It's like a party with everybody in town invited. Close to the church itself are booths run by the local people: Martha Peabody sells boxes of molasses cookies . . . LuElla Quinn raffles off the quilt she spent the whole winter stitching together . . . the Reverend Terwilliger sets up a scale and tries to guess people's weight. That kind of thing.

But away off at the far end of the lawn, down by the clump of birch trees, is a space where "outsiders" can set up booths—if they pay the church ten dollars for the privilege. Sometimes there's a woman selling hats with your name sewn onto the brim, or a couple who run a penny toss with balloons for prizes. And once there was a man who heated bits of glass and shaped them into animals you could buy for a dollar or two.

The story of The Wish Giver begins on one such Saturday, with me wandering about, sampling a piece of cake here, and admiring some homemade jewelry there, and taking a general delight in seeing all the villagers decked out in their best clothes.

At first the ragged, mildew-spotted tent down

under the birch trees seemed like nothing more than a mound of earth with canvas thrown over it. I must have walked by it two or three times before even noticing the little sign hanging out in front:

THADDEUS BLINN

I CAN GIVE YOU

WHATEVER

YOU ASK FOR

ONLY 50¢

Impossible, I thought. Suppose I asked Thaddeus Blinn to cure my knee that got sore whenever the weather changed, or I wanted the hair to grow back on my bald spot. Fiddlesticks! I started to walk away.

"There are no limits, you know. Anything you could possibly imagine can be yours."

I turned about. The man who'd drawn back the tent flaps was short and fat, like a big ball on two legs. He wore a white suit, and his vest was red, with a thick gold watch chain stretched across his belly. The huge mustache under his bulb of a nose bristled fiercely as his mouth curved into a toothy smile. He put me in mind of Santa Claus, shaved and dressed for warm weather.

"Blinn's the name, sir," he said with a tip of his derby. "Thaddeus Blinn, at your service."

Something happened then that might have been just my imagining or a trick of the light. Thaddeus Blinn's eyes *glowed* for a brief moment, like those of a cat when lantern light reaches the dark corner where it's sitting. Even after the glow died, Blinn's eyes didn't appear quite human. The pupils weren't round, but long and narrow like the eyes of a snake.

"If you don't come inside now, you'll not sleep tonight from wondering about me, Stew Meat," Blinn went on.

I forgot all about his eyes when I heard that. "How in tarnation did you know my name?" I asked him.

"Your curiosity will soon be satisfied," said Blinn, pointing into the tent.

It was cool and shady inside, with the air full of the musty smell of old canvas. A bench ran across the rear of the tent, and three people were sitting on it.

Eleven-year-old Polly Kemp was at one end.

Polly lives with her widowed mother out where the footbridge crosses Spider Crick. If Polly'd lived closer to town where she ran into folks more often, there's a real possibility that somebody in a fit of anger would have done her real bodily harm. Or at least put a muzzle on her.

Not that Polly was downright mean. She just said whatever popped into her head without a thought about whether the words she said hurt others. Honesty, Polly called it. But when honesty causes nothing but anger and hurt feelings, maybe there ought to be a limit. Polly, though, didn't know what that limit was.

Next to Polly was Rowena Jervis. A giddy fifteen, Rowena was in love with love itself. She had her eye on Henry Piper, the young farm-machinery salesman who came to town twice a year. He'd make eyes at Rowena, and she'd go all soft inside and sigh deeply and write "Mrs. Henry Piper" in the dust on my store window. If Rowena had a wish granted by Thaddeus Blinn, then Henry Piper would be in it somewhere.

A little apart from the two girls was sixteen-year-old Adam Fiske. His pa's farm was the driest in the county, and when there were spells of no rain, Adam spent a lot of his time toting water all the way from Spider Crick in his wagon with the tubs in back. Just now, after three weeks without rain, Adam would probably have given everything he possessed for a single glass of water that he didn't have to haul all the way from that durned crick.

I took a seat between Rowena and Adam. We all looked up at Blinn. The little man stood at the entrance of the tent, and he seemed to be hoping more customers would come along.

"I've been here nearly half an hour," said Adam finally. "Can we get on with it, Mr. Blinn?"

"I should think so," Polly added. "I ain't planning on sitting in this smelly tent all day."

Thaddeus Blinn let the tent flaps fall and turned toward us. The expression on his face showed he wasn't too happy about having so few of us there. "Alas!" he said with a sigh. "So many people just cannot make themselves believe."

"I'm not really sure I believe you myself," said Rowena. "I read the sign and just came in because I was curious. What is it you're selling, Mr. Blinn?"

"I'm selling wishes, child." Blinn spread his hands as if it was the most obvious thing in the world. "Anything you want—anything you could possibly imagine—can be yours!"

All of us on the bench looked at one another, and Polly kind of giggled. I wondered if Mr. Blinn was crazy in the head.

"I would love to get a wish," Rowena said. "But it all sounds so . . . so incredible."

"I deal in the incredible," Blinn replied with a vast grin. "But before I go further, I must have my fee. Fifty cents from each of you, if you please."

"And just what are we buying here?" I asked.

"You'll see, Stew Meat," Blinn answered. "It'll be well worth your money, I promise you that."

With some reluctance, we all dug down into pockets and purses. Blinn moved his hand along like a church collection plate, and when he'd finished, it was full of coins. He thrust the coins deep into his pocket. When his hand came out of the pocket again, it held four little white cards. Each card had a red spot on it. Blinn gave one of the cards to each of us.

"It doesn't seem like I'm getting much for my fifty cents," I said to Adam. He chuckled along with me.

"With that card, Stew Meat, you have all the

incredible forces of the universe at your command!" Blinn said the words like he was announcing the end of the world.

"Horsefeathers!" cried Polly. "My ma worked awful hard so I'd have fifty cents for the Church Social. Now you've got it, and all I have is this worthless card."

"Worthless?" exclaimed Blinn. "How dare you say that, girl!"

"I've got a mind to fetch the sheriff and have you jailed," Polly went on. "What use do I have for a dumb card with a spot on it?"

"Come now, Mr. Blinn," said Adam. "You can't expect us to believe . . ."

"I *do* expect you to believe," said Blinn. "You see, I am—for lack of a better term—a giver of wishes. To be more accurate, I am *The* Wish Giver, as to my knowledge there is no other."

"And these cards are supposed to make our wishes come true?" asked Rowena. "That's mighty hard to swallow."

"The card will bring you anything your heart could desire," said Blinn peevishly. The fact that none of us believed or trusted him seemed to drive the little man frantic. "Anything. Wealth . . . beauty . . . fame. Just wish, and it

---

will be yours. But each card can grant only a single wish, so think carefully before making it."

"I'll tell you what I'm thinking," Polly piped up. "I think we've been cheated. If you can grant all kinds of wishes, how come you're selling these cards for fifty cents? All you'd have to do is wish for—"

"I have no need for money," Blinn replied, "except as a sign of the good faith of my customers. What I crave is respect . . . appreciation . . . recognition. Look about you and consider. Of all the people at the Social today, only you four were curious enough . . . imaginative enough . . . yes, even courageous enough . . . to hear me out. Oh, the shame, that my talents should be taken so lightly." The words tumbled out of Thaddeus Blinn's mouth like wasps from a burning nest. He finally pulled himself together, though, and spoke a bit more slowly.

"You four shall be rewarded for your trust in me. When you're ready, you have only to press your thumb against the red spot on the card and utter your wish aloud. The wish—one wish only, for each of you—will be granted."

"Then I wish for . . ." Adam Fiske began.

———

"Wait, lad! Wait!" Blinn warned him. "Take your time. Give it plenty of thought."

Polly glared at Blinn and muttered something about wanting her money back. Rowena stared doubtfully at the red spot, and Adam shook his head as he slipped the card into his pocket. For a moment Blinn stared down at us. A toothy smile drifted across his face. Then he rushed to the end of the tent and threw open the flaps.

"Now you have what you came for," he announced in a singsong voice. "It's time for me to be on my way. Outside, please. Everybody out."

I guess all four of us were thinking the same thing—that Thaddeus Blinn was a fast-talking fraud who wanted to be far away from Coven Tree when we found out the wish cards didn't work.

We shuffled out into the warm sunlight. "Take great care when you wish," Blinn called after us. "For it will be granted exactly as you ask for it."

"You can bet one thing, Mr. Blinn," said Adam Fiske. "If this wishing business really works, I'll be coming back for another card the next time you're in town."

"Alas!" Blinn replied. "I travel each road but once. Always I must seek out new places and new faces. Once we part, we will never meet again."

Once more I thought I saw that glow in Blinn's eyes, just before he snapped the tent flaps tight shut like a magician doing a disappearing act. That was the last we ever saw of the strange little man, Thaddeus Blinn.

Rowena and Polly and Adam and I went our separate ways after that. I returned to the store and slipped my card into the back of the cash register as a souvenir of fifty cents foolishly spent.

Once back in familiar surroundings, I couldn't help chuckling at myself and the awe I'd felt when I first met Thaddeus Blinn. Perhaps he'd heard someone greet me on the church lawn, and that's how he'd learned my name. His glowing eyes had been only a trick played by the bright sunshine, and their odd shape just showed I needed glasses.

By the time I'd prepared my supper, I was certain that fat, eager-to-please Thaddeus Blinn was nothing more than a crafty humbug. He earned his livelihood by selling little white cards and incredible dreams. And if the dreams didn't come true, that sly buzzard would be long gone by the time folks found out.

But what a story ol' Thaddeus Blinn had told us! He must have convinced those three young folks that at least a part of the things he said were true. For a while there in the tent, he'd almost had me believing it myself. . . .

Jug-a-Rum

On the bank of Spider Crick, Polly Kemp bent down and grasped the wide cattail leaf. Leland Wickstaff and his twin sister Lenora stood on either side of her with big grins on their faces. Polly pulled the leaf back slowly.

There sat a bullfrog nearly the size of a soup plate. Its shiny green-and-black skin glistened in the setting sun, and its wide eyes stared straight ahead. Then the loose skin beneath the frog's throat began to puff up like a ball as air was gulped into it. The huge mouth opened wide.

JUG-A-RUM!

"I knowed you'd find that critter if you looked hard enough," crowed Leland. "You done real good, Polly!"

The frog raised its head, startled by the shout.

Suddenly its powerful hind legs shot out, launching it into a long dive over the water. It landed with a loud *plop* and disappeared.

"Consarn you, Leland Wickstaff!" Polly howled. "I didn't spend all this time looking for that frog just so you could scare it off! I wanted to watch it awhile and maybe see it catch a fly with its long tongue. Then you start to bellering and make it jump off, and there ain't enough sun left to go find another one. Why, you haven't got the sense you was born with. If brains were—"

Splat

A big gob of mud hit Polly right in the middle of her back. She spun about just in time to see Lenora scoop up another handful and hurl it at her. Polly dodged, and the mud spattered against a tree.

"You stop that, Lenora!" she cried. "I was talking to Leland, not you. It ain't fair, each of you siding with the other whenever—"

Splat

This time it was Leland who threw the mud. It struck Polly on the ankle, and she could feel it run down into her shoe.

"Let's play by ourselves, Lenora," said Leland. "Just us two."

"Good idea," Lenora replied. "We can make like Polly just vanished."

"Don't you two dare pull a trick like that!"

Polly looked from one of the Wickstaff twins to the other. It was hard to tell them apart, especially now in the twilight. Both wore blue overalls and checkered shirts. Both had freckles, and hair the color of ripe wheat. The only difference was, Lenora's hair was in braids, while Leland's looked like somebody'd put a bowl on his head and clipped away all the hair sticking out from under it.

Lenora and Leland lived with their ma and pa in an old shanty down where the crick formed a big pond. Neither twin was any great shakes in school, but what they didn't know about the mountains and woods and streams around Coven Tree wasn't worth knowing. They were as shy as wild foxes most of the time. But if an argument or a fight started, you couldn't take on just one of the twins without having to answer to both of 'em. And Lenora was just as handy with either words or fists as her brother.

21

Usually, though, they kept apart from other people, content with one another's company. Polly was proud and happy that she'd been able to make friends with them several months ago.

It had all started the day Polly found the crow with the broken wing. She was carrying it home when she met the twins on the path.

"Whatcha got there, Polly?" Leland asked.

"A crow that's been hurt. I'm going to figure some way to fix its wing bone. Then I'll split its tongue and—"

"Split its tongue?" Leland exclaimed. "What for?"

"I've heard tell that when you split a crow's tongue, it'll talk real words. I'm going to try it."

"No bird'll talk when you split its tongue," scoffed Lenora. "Most likely you'll kill it. Leland, show Polly how to set that wing bone."

The twins helped Polly set the wing and bandaged it tight to the crow's body before leaving for home. The following day, much to Polly's surprise, Leland and Lenora showed up bright and early, asking about the bird. In the weeks that followed, they took Polly along on their treks through the woods, one day searching out fiddler ferns, and another locating a bee tree. Lenora even showed Polly how to catch a trout with just a few pieces of yarn tied to a hook. By the time the crow was ready to be returned to the wild, Polly and the twins were close friends.

Sometimes, however, Polly's mouth got in the way of their friendship. But unlike the village children, the twins didn't just walk off when Polly's mouth got the best of her. Leland and Lenora believed in getting even.

Once Polly was yammering at Leland for pretending they'd gotten lost in a deep part of the forest. Right in the middle of her angry shouting, Lenora sneaked up and dropped a little green snake down the collar of her shirt. Another time, when a wasp stung Lenora and Polly jeered at her cries of pain, the twins picked her up and tossed her in the crick, clothes and all.

This time they'd thrown mud. Now they stood at the edge of the woods, and Leland grinned at his sister.

"Ain't it nice, being way out here, Lenora?" he said. "Just the two of us."

"It sure is," Lenora replied. "No Polly Kemp around with her infernal jabbering."

"You're talking like I was a mile away," said Polly angrily. "I'm standing right here talking to you."

"Did you hear something, Lenora?" Leland asked.

"Yeah," said his sister. "It must have been an ol' froggy down in the swamp."

"I ain't no . . ." howled Polly. But then the tone of her voice changed. "I don't want you to stay mad at me," she went on softly.

"That frog's sounding more human all the time," said Leland.

"I . . . I'm sorry I talked that way. Please come back."

Lenora turned about. "Well I'll be . . . That ain't no frog, Leland. It's Polly Kemp. What are you doing out here, Polly?"

Polly knew the twins were teasing her, but she didn't say a word. She didn't want them to walk away again.

"I didn't see either of you at the Church Social," she began finally. "I looked everywhere for you."

"We didn't go," Leland told her. "Everybody expects you to spend money there. I feel funny when I don't have any to spend."

"And I don't like all the girls in their fancy dresses laughing at me 'cause all I've got to wear is overalls," said Lenora.

"We'll listen if you want to tell us about it." Leland tried to act bored, but Polly could tell that both twins were eager to hear what went on.

"It was fair to middling," she began. "The booths were real pretty, and there was lots of nice things for sale. But most folks acted like they usually do, either real uppity or else staring right through me like I was invisible or something. Mrs. Peabody carried on something fierce just because I said her cookies tasted like biting into a sofa pillow."

The twins giggled. Then Lenora stuck her nose in the air and stuck out a limp-wristed hand. "I suppose," she said, trying to act real fancy, "that Agatha Benthorn and Eunice Ingersoll were there."

"Stop that, Lenora!" Polly snapped. "Just because I'm trying to make friends with Agatha and Eunice, you've got no call to make fun of me."

"Them two ain't nothing but frilly little skunkweeds," said Leland. "If we show 'em something we found in the woods, or just walk up and talk to them, they get all high-and-mighty and treat us like we were nothing but a bushel of dirt."

"Do you think they'd want to see that frog you found?" added Lenora. "I guess not. One look, and they'd go scooting off with their noses in the air and holding their lacy skirts high so's not to get any dirt on them. You just ain't their kind, Polly. And you should be thankful for that."

"They never so much as give you the time of day," said Leland. "So why you keep chasing after those stuck-up little prigs is beyond me."

"They're quality folks!" said Polly. "And rich, too. I plan to be just like them someday. I'll live in the biggest house in Coven Tree and buy everything I ever wanted and—"

"I think you've gone fuzzy in the head," Leland declared.

"I ain't. You'll see."

"Agatha and Eunice are too dumb to enjoy the woods and the crick and the things we like," snorted Lenora with a toss of her head. "All they like to do is sit on silk pillows and talk about the latest fashions and drink weak tea and . . .

26

Yucck! Come on, Leland. Let's go home."

Off they went, leaving Polly standing in the red twilight.

It was dark by the time Polly got home. She entered the living room, and her mother looked up from the lapful of clothes she was sewing and mending for the Coven Tree ladies who had neither the time nor the skill.

"You're late," Mrs. Kemp said. "How are Leland and Lenora?"

"Consarn those two. I don't care what they think. I don't care what anybody thinks. I'm going to make friends with Agatha and Eunice if it kills me. Then folks will sit up and take notice of me, all right!"

The next day—Sunday—everybody in Coven Tree was all togged out in fine fashion for going to church. The women had on bright dresses, and the men wore suits and ties, sometimes tugging at collars that were too tight.

Agatha Benthorn looked pretty enough to gladden the heart of an angel. Her hair was curled, and she wore a new dress covered with lace. Around her waist was a wide pink ribbon, tied in back with a bow.

———

27

The service went just fine, with the Reverend Terwilliger preaching a sermon that must have had the Devil shaking in his boots. It wasn't until afterward that the trouble started. When Agatha came outside, Polly was right behind her.

Agatha rushed down the steps to greet Eunice Ingersoll. At the same time Polly reached out and took hold of one of the loops of the pink ribbon bow. There was a loud ripping sound. Agatha stood at the bottom of the steps with the bow of her dress all ragged and torn. Polly was at the top, with a big piece of ribbon in her fist.

One look at Polly and you could see how sorry she was for what she'd done. She opened her mouth, but no words came out.

Then Agatha ran up the steps to Polly and slapped her right across the face—hard!

"Agatha, I . . . I . . ."

If Polly didn't have any words, Agatha sure did. "You wretched thing!" she spat. "You tore my beautiful dress, you . . . you ragamuffin! Of all the spiteful—"

"Agatha, if you'll just—"

"No!" Agatha leveled a finger at Polly the way she might have pointed a pistol. "You are dirt, Polly Kemp! You are dirt, and everything that's horrid. There's not a person in town who wants anything to do with you. So just stay away from me, do you hear? Stay away!"

Off went Agatha, leaving Polly red-eyed and almost crying. She just wanted to be friends with Agatha . . . and now the thing seemed spoiled beyond repair.

Polly moped about the house all day, and her mother wondered if she was coming down with some illness. Evening came and Polly trudged up to her room to do her homework. Outside, down by Spider Crick, the frogs began their shrill chirping and peeping.

Chirp-a-chirp! Chirp-a-chirp!

To Polly it sounded like: Ag-a-tha! Ag-a-tha!

And then a deep bullfrog's croak, like the string of a bass fiddle being plucked.

JUG-A-RUM!

Suddenly Polly got up from her chair. She walked to the little table near the window. There, just as she'd left it after the Church Social, was the card with the red circle on it.

In the twilight, Polly turned the card over and over in her hands. Oh, it was foolish of course. Yet she'd paid her fifty cents. Thaddeus Blinn had told her that whatever she asked for would

------

29

be hers. What was the harm in trying?

Carefully she placed her right thumb over the red circle. "I want ever so badly to be liked," she said softly. "And not just by Leland and Lenora, either. I want people to greet me and not walk on the other side of the street whenever they set eyes on me. And especially I want Agatha Benthorn to invite me to her house for tea.

"So that's what I'm wishing for, Mr. Wish Giver. I'm wishing that people will pay attention to me. And smile when they see me. And I wish that someday soon, Agatha will ask me to come to her house. I know I'm a fool for believing Thaddeus Blinn is anything but a fake, but . . ."

Suddenly Polly dropped the card. That was funny. The red spot felt warm—almost hot—against her thumb. She looked down at the floor, and a little gasp escaped from her throat.

The card had fallen under the bed, away from the light of the tiny lamp. In the darkness the spot on the card glowed like a burning coal.

Outside her window the sound of the frogs could still be heard.

Chirp-a-chirp! Chirp-a-chirp!
Ag-a-tha! Ag-a-tha!
JUG-A-RUM!

Polly tossed and turned in her bed until late that night. She couldn't get her mind off Agatha and the torn dress. The frogs down by Spider Crick kept up their chirping and croaking. Finally in the small hours of the morning, Polly nodded off.

She woke up just shy of eight o'clock. She was still tired, and her eyes felt like they had sand in them. Polly washed herself, combed her hair, and got dressed, feeling meaner than a snapping turtle on account of not sleeping well. She trudged downstairs and into the kitchen.

Mrs. Kemp sighed and shook her head when she saw the mood Polly was in and hoped her daughter would hold off any complaining until she got to school. But Polly took one look at her toast and eggs and started in.

"Mother, the toast is just horrid. It's all burned and—

"JUG-A-RUM!"

How on earth could a bullfrog have gotten into the house? Mrs. Kemp wondered. Why, it sounded like it was right in the kitchen.

"JUG-A-RUM!"

Mrs. Kemp's eyes lit on Polly. The girl was sitting bolt upright with one hand at her throat. She looked like she was about to scream, but the sound that came out was:

"JUG-A-RUM!"

Polly's mother shook her head in exasperation. "You can stop that right now, young lady," she said. "Making frog sounds isn't going to get you out of school today. You've told me you were sick too many other times, and then—"

"JUG-A-RUM! JUG-A-RUM!"

"That's enough, Polly!"

"JUG-A-RUM!"

"All right, be a frog if you want to. But get that breakfast into you and be off."

Before she knew it, Polly was standing on the front steps with her coat on and her schoolbooks under her arm. Her mother slammed the door behind her.

33

Polly shuffled down the road to school, scared to death by the croaks that come from her mouth when she tried to speak. Once or twice she tried talking to herself, unable to believe what had happened.

"JUG-A-RUM!"

When she was about halfway to school, she heard running footsteps on the path behind her. She turned around, and there was Adam Fiske. She hoped he'd just pass on without saying anything, but as he came up beside her, he slowed to a walk.

"Good morning, Polly," said Adam. "After today I've got a few days off before final tests start. What do you think of that?"

Polly didn't like it at all. The older students were lucky. She still had to go to school every day.

"JUG-A-RUM!"

"You don't have to get sassy with me, Polly Kemp," Adam told her.

"JUG-A-RUM!"

Adam stopped walking and looked carefully at Polly. "Hey, you do that real good. It sounds just like a bullfrog."

"JUG-A-RUM!"

34

"I've got better things to do than talk to some-body who only makes frog sounds," said Adam. " 'Bye, Froggy." And he trotted off down the road.

When Polly reached the school playground, the first thing she saw was Agatha Benthorn standing near the swings whispering something into Eunice Ingersoll's ear. Eunice pointed, and Agatha turned about. She made an ugly face at Polly and stuck out her tongue. Then she and Eunice linked arms and walked away with their heads high, leaving Polly behind, unable to say a word.

It wasn't fair, Polly thought miserably. She hadn't intended to say anything peevish or nasty. Instead, she wanted to tell Agatha how sorry she was about tearing the dress. But all she could do was croak, and if the two girls heard her, they'd laugh. Polly didn't think she could stand that.

"For once you kept your mouth shut," she heard someone say, "instead of letting it get you into trouble. Good for you, Polly."

It was Lenora Wickstaff. Leland was with her. Polly tried to speak.

"JUG-A-RUM!"

"You sound just like a bullfrog," said Leland

with a big grin on his face. "Where'd you learn to do that, Polly? Can you teach us?"

"JUG-A-RUM! JUG-A-RUM!"

"Leland's talking to you, Polly," said Lenora. "Can't you do anything but croak at him?"

"JUG-A-RUM!"

Leland and Lenora looked at one another in astonishment. They led Polly to a quiet corner of the playground. "Say something, Polly," Lenora ordered in a hushed voice. "Like . . . what's your name?"

"JUG-A-RUM!"

"Come on, Polly," said Leland. "Stop fooling around."

"She's not fooling, you dumb lummox," Lenora told her brother. "Nobody fools with tears running down their face. Polly, what's happened?"

"JUG-A-RUM!"

"Here, dry your eyes." Lenora took a handkerchief from her pocket and started scrubbing at Polly's face.

When the school doors opened, Lenora and Leland stood close beside Polly and pretended to be talking to her and listening to her. Polly got to her room just as the teacher, Miss Morasco, was about to call the roll.

"Robert Appleton?"

"Here."

"Agatha Benthorn?"

"Here."

Polly gazed miserably at the floor. Soon her name would be called. She'd have to answer. Already she could imagine the whole class laughing at her.

"Eunice Ingersoll?"

"Here."

"Polly Kemp?"

Polly waved her hand about frantically. Miss Morasco just had to see she was in her seat. Maybe the teacher wouldn't ask . . .

"Polly Kemp?" Miss Morasco looked up from the class list in her hand. "Polly," she said, "the rule is clear. To be marked present, you must answer 'Here' when I call your name."

Silently Polly nodded her head. A boy chuckled, and Agatha Benthorn leaned toward Eunice Ingersoll. "First time I ever saw Polly Kemp without any words to say," Agatha told Eunice.

Polly heard the remark. She was so outraged she didn't even think about croaking.

"Here!" said Polly loudly.

Miss Morasco nodded and went on with the roll call.

Polly couldn't believe what had happened. Somehow she could talk again!

For the whole morning Polly didn't say much, and what she did say was in a whisper. But the croaking seemed to have completely disappeared. Just before lunch she was able to give Miss Morasco the capitals of all the states with only two mistakes.

On the playground the boys were hogging both swings and even the seesaw. It made Polly angry. She was about to shout at them to give the girls a turn, when Leland Wickstaff grabbed her arm and led her to a corner of the school yard where Lenora was sitting.

"You look meaner than a snake with the toothache, Polly," Leland said. "But don't start in yelling. Maybe shouting is what made you lose your voice in the first place."

"I'm just glad it's over," said Lenora. "When did the croaking start, Polly?"

"This morning," Polly replied. "I was eating breakfast, and I was right in the middle of complaining to mother about how she'd burned the toast when—"

"If I complained to my ma about burned toast, she'd whack my backside," Leland told her.

"You just give your voice a rest, Polly," said Lenora. "Miss Morasco said it was real nice, the way you've been so polite all morning. She told me she'd never seen you like this before."

Polly smiled. She liked hearing that Miss Morasco was pleased with her.

After lunch was arithmetic class. It was Polly's best subject.

Agatha Benthorn was sent to the blackboard to do a multiplication problem. Her hand shook as she wrote the numbers. Everybody in Coven Tree knew Agatha didn't know beans about arithmetic.

"Seven times seven is seventy-seven," Agatha mumbled to herself.

Polly's hand shot up. "Seven times seven ain . . . isn't . . . seventy-seven," she called out. "It's forty-nine."

"Quite right," said Miss Morasco. "Someone else had better finish up, Agatha."

Agatha slunk back to her seat. Polly leaned over and patted her shoulder comfortingly.

"Don't feel bad," Polly said. "Anybody could make—"

"Don't you say a word, you . . . you urchin!" Agatha whispered. "Maybe you know your numbers, but you're trash, and that's all you'll ever be!"

Well, that tore it! Nobody—*nobody*—talked to Polly that way.

"Agatha Benthorn, you are dumb!" shouted Polly, not caring who heard her. "You ain't got the sense that—

"JUG-A-RUM!"

Everybody in the class looked around to see where the frog was.

"JUG-A-RUM! JUG-A-RUM!"

It was happening again!

"It's Polly Kemp!" howled a skinny boy in the back row. "Polly sounds like a bullfrog!"

The other pupils were pointing their fingers at her and laughing. Polly couldn't stand it.

"JUG-A-RUM!" she shouted.

The laughing and jeering got louder.

"Stop it at once!" At the sound of Miss Morasco's voice, the students became as still as stones.

"Polly, are you croaking like that on purpose?" the teacher asked.

Polly shook her head. *"JUG-A-RUM!"*

"Come to my desk, Polly," said Miss Morasco.

41

Moments later Polly was trudging along the path to her house. When she arrived, she gave her mother the note Miss Morasco had written. Mrs. Kemp read the note and then tried to ask Polly some questions, but the only answer she got was:

"JUG-A-RUM!"

Mrs. Kemp gave Polly some hot tea and then sent her to bed, promising to call the doctor if she wasn't better in the morning.

Lying there with the thick quilt wrapped around her, Polly tried to figure out what was happening to her. She thought about it for nearly an hour without any success at all. "I . . . I don't want to sound like a bullfrog all the time," she whimpered.

She sat up and stared at her reflection in the mirror on the far wall. She'd talked—she'd said real words!

"Mother!" she called. "Mother, the bullfrog sound is gone. I can talk again!"

Mrs. Kemp came a-running. "It must have been my tea," she said. "Strong tea is good for whatever ails a body."

For the rest of the day Polly talked a blue streak, the words just tumbling from her mouth.

42

After school the Wickstaff twins came by to see how she was feeling.

"The croaking went away," she told them. "I'm cured."

"Yeah," said Lenora doubtfully. "Maybe."

"No maybe about it," Polly answered. "Listen to me talk."

"Polly, you were croaking when you came to school," said Lenora. "Then you could talk again. Then it was back to the croaking."

"But now it's all gone," said Polly. "I'm all better."

"The croaking happened twice," said Leland. "Who's to say it won't start up again, just when you least expect it?"

Leland was right! The croaking might begin again!

"Ohhhhh!" Polly groaned.

"And there's another problem," said Leland. "You'd best tell it Lenora. You're the one who heard it."

"What problem?" asked Polly.

"Well," Lenora began, "I overheard Agatha and Eunice talking together after school. They're up to something, Polly—something to do with you. They were saying how they were

---

43

going to do something to get even with you for tearing Agatha's dress and for what you said to her in school."

That was the end of Polly's happy feeling. The croaking might come back at any time. And on top of that, Agatha and Eunice were plotting against her.

That night in bed, Polly lay sobbing into her pillow. Suddenly she shifted her head, listening.

She'd often heard the sound before. But then it had come from off in the direction of Spider Crick. Now, however, it was right outside her window.

Chirp-a-chirp! Chirp-a-chirp!
JUG-A-RUM!

Frogs! Thousands of them. And from the sound, they were just outside in the yard, each one talking to her in its own way.

Chirp-a-chirp! Chirp-a-chirp!
JUG-A-RUM!

All that long night Polly tossed and turned and dreamed of big, slimy bullfrogs climbing in through her window and snuggling their wet bodies next to hers under the blankets.

Polly woke at first light. The frogs had gone back to their swamp, and the only light in the room was the faint glow of dawn showing through the window.

She sat up in bed, clutching the quilt about her neck. For the first time she could remember, Polly was deep-down scared. Twice yesterday, the only sound she had been able to make was a bullfrog's deep *jug-a-rum.* Even now she was afraid to open her mouth for fear that the frog sound would come out.

What made it happen? It wasn't any disease she'd ever heard of. And she didn't think she was going crazy.

"What a terrible thing," she said softly. Then she breathed a sigh of relief. At least for now, she had the power of speech.

But she couldn't go on like this for the rest of her life, making *jug-a-rum* sounds every now and then and who-knew-when. There had to be some reason for it. And if she could think of the reason, she might be able to do something about it.

So Polly made it a point to say "hello" to everyone she met on the way to school that morning. That startled folks, because it wasn't like Polly Kemp to be so pleasant. They didn't know it was just her way of reassuring herself that she could still talk.

Leland and Lenora were waiting for her on the playground. "Looks like your croaking ain't the only strange thing going on in Coven Tree," said Leland.

"We came crosslots, behind Rowena Jervis's house," Lenora added. "Rowena was up early."

"Let me tell it," interrupted Leland. "Y'see, Polly, Rowena was standing in the middle of that little grove of trees out in back of her house. She seemed to be talking to somebody. But as far as we could see, there wasn't anybody with her. Just a bunch of trees. Can you imagine anybody standing and talking to a tree?"

It did sound odd to Polly. When they'd sat together in the tent at the Church Social, Rowena had seemed perfectly all right. What could have started her to jabbering away to trees?

Odd . . . strange . . .

More pupils arrived. They began crowding around Polly, hoping she'd make frog sounds again. But as soon as they heard her speaking normally, they lost interest and went to play on the swings and slides. The morning lessons went by quickly, with Miss Morasco calling on Polly three times and Polly knowing each of the answers.

Then came noon recess. All the boys and girls went out on the playground after lunch, and Polly wanted to swing. But when she got there, both swings were taken, with Charlie Peabody on one and Alfred Dawes on the other. So Polly sat to one side to wait her turn.

But Charlie and Alfred stayed on those swings. And stayed and stayed. Every once in a while they'd glance over to where Polly was sitting, and they'd kind of laugh behind their hands. They knew they were getting her riled.

Charlie called to her. "Bet you'd like to swing, wouldn't you, Polly? But you ain't gonna do it today. Maybe not tomorrow, either. Us boys need the swings, and you're nothing but a dumb girl."

Polly wasn't about to listen to that kind of talk. "Charlie Peabody!" she shouted, angry as anything. "You are a big hunk of nothing. And you too, Alfred. You two big gobs of mud ain't got even the leftover brains that was given to boys after the girls got the good ones. And if you two dunderheads don't—

"JUG-A-RUM!"

Polly clapped her hands over her mouth. Too late! Everybody on the playground looked over at her, and suddenly there wasn't a sound to be heard. Miss Morasco rushed to Polly's side.

"Are you all right?" the teacher asked.

Polly didn't know whether to try and speak or just shake her head. Suddenly Lenora Wickstaff was standing there and talking to Miss Morasco in a whisper.

"Polly ain't feeling quite up to snuff," Lenora said. "But she'll be all right if the others'll leave her alone for a while."

"Well, I . . ." Miss Morasco began doubtfully. Then she nodded. "Very well, Lenora."

Leland walked up and led Polly to a bench in the corner of the yard. "We'll care for her, ma'am," he said. "Don't worry."

While the rest of the students were herded to the other side of the playground, the twins got Polly calmed down to a point where she'd listen to what they wanted to tell her.

"Lenora thinks she knows what's making you start in croaking," said Leland. "It don't sound likely to me, but . . . well, you tell it, Lenora."

"Polly," she said, "you told me that when it happened the first time—yesterday morning at breakfast—you were complaining to your mother about some burned toast."

Polly nodded, trying to hold back her tears.

"When you get to complaining, you can say some pretty mean things, Polly Kemp."

Polly remembered how annoyed she'd been by the burned toast. She'd told her mother . . . Again she nodded, completely ashamed of herself.

"And the second time," Lenora went on, "you'd just said to Agatha Benthorn that she was . . ."

Dumb . . . Polly clearly recalled saying the spiteful word.

"Don't you see, Polly? Just now you were in the middle of telling Charlie and Alfred what you thought of 'em, and it happened again. It appears like every time you start giving somebody what for, some kind of power pulls you up short and makes you begin croaking instead of talking."

"It seems that after a while, though," Leland said, "the thing wears off, and you can speak human words again."

Polly stared from Lenora to Leland and back again. It was impossible! Yet what other explanation could there be?

"Trouble is," said Lenora, "there's no telling what brought this thing on you now. You've been speaking your mind to people and snapping and snarling for years, but this is the first time . . ."

But Polly knew why it was different now. She thought back to Sunday evening when she'd made the wish on the red spot. What had she said?

I'm wishing that people will pay attention to me. And smile when they see me.

That part had come true, right enough. When Polly started *jug-a-rum*ing in school, she'd gotten plenty of attention. More than she'd really cared for. As for the smiling, most of the pupils had been laughing right out loud.

But there was another part to her wish, too:

. . . That someday soon, Agatha will ask me to come to her house.

At least that part wouldn't come true, thought Polly. Maybe it was for the best. If she got to croaking at Agatha's house, and if Agatha and Eunice laughed at her again the way they had in school, she didn't know what she'd do.

The thought of what had happened set Polly's head to spinning dizzily. She couldn't help wondering how things would be from now on. There was no possibility of unwishing what she'd asked for. Thaddeus Blinn had left Coven Tree, never to return. She'd be like this forever, forced to say only whipped-cream compliments and sweet things to people, no matter how horrid they were. Either that or begin the ridiculous croaking.

By the end of the lunch hour Polly was again able to speak. Miss Morasco looked her over carefully and even made her recite "Peter Piper Picked a Peck of Pickled Peppers" before she was allowed to go to her seat. All afternoon Polly sat mute, considering the mess she'd made of things with her wish.

Perhaps if she were to tell Agatha Benthorn

how sorry she was for the wretched things she'd done and said, maybe Thaddeus Blinn would take pity on her and remove the magic spell. It was just a forlorn hope, but at least it was better than nothing.

How to go about it was the problem. Agatha certainly wouldn't talk to Polly at school, and it would be impossible to see Agatha at home. No children ever went inside the big house on the hill except Eunice Ingersoll. The two girls would sip tea and eat little cookies and act like real ladies.

But before they could have their tea, they'd have to get the little cookies. They bought fresh ones every day. Before going home, Agatha would stop at the only place in Coven Tree where the cookies were sold—Stew Meat's store!

At dismissal Polly dashed out of school and ran across the playground as fast as she could. She tried to get straight all the things she was going to say. But no matter how she arranged them, they never seemed to sound right.

Polly got to the store first. She was hiding behind a display of canned goods when Agatha and Eunice walked in the front door, gossiping to one another. While the two purchased their

cookies, Polly started summoning up the nerve to step out and show herself.

She'd just about got her courage up, when suddenly she began listening to what Agatha and Eunice were saying to one another.

"I don't know what's come over her," said Agatha. "Croaking like that, and right in school. Imagine! Do you suppose she's doing it on purpose?"

"I don't think she can help it," replied Eunice with a little giggle. "Polly wouldn't want folks laughing at her the way they do when she makes that sound."

"Serves the little wretch right! After what she did to my dress and all."

Then a big grin spread across Agatha's face. "I can hardly wait until Thursday."

"Do you suppose she'll accept your invitation?" asked Eunice.

"Of course she will. She's been simply dying to come to my house for ages." Then Agatha began whispering in Eunice's ear.

"Fix her once and for all . . . be really funny . . . my mother will . . ."

"What a marvelous idea," said Eunice finally. Both girls started giggling like little imps.

Polly slipped out the back of the store. She knew that she—and *JUG-A-RUM!*—were the cause of the girls' laughter. Well, she'd be hanged if she'd give Agatha and Eunice the satisfaction of humiliating her even more.

Then Polly's stubborn pride took over. No, she'd accept the invitation. Even if they were plotting against her, she'd show them she could be a real lady even if . . . if she croaked like a frog until she was old and gray.

She ran around the outside of the store and came in through the front door, looking for all the world as if she'd just arrived from school. "Hello, Agatha . . . Eunice," she said as politely as she could.

Both girls greeted her like a long-lost friend. "How wonderful to see you, Polly," Agatha purred.

"And how well you're looking," cooed Eunice.

"There's something I've been meaning to ask you, Polly," Agatha said. "And I guess this is a good time to do it."

So in spite of everything, the last part of the wish is to be granted, thought Polly. But she managed to keep the butter-wouldn't-melt-in-my-mouth expression on her face.

"Ask me? Ask me what, Agatha?"

"Polly dear, how would you like to join Eunice and me for tea on Thursday? After school? At my house?"

The next day—Wednesday—Polly made up her mind that she was going to be friendly if it killed her. There was no way anybody was going to make her say anything mean and start croaking again.

The first person she met as she walked onto the playground was Olivia Heidecker. As Polly came toward her, Olivia started to walk away.

"I like that dress you're wearing, Olivia," said Polly. "Them ruffles at the shoulders are real pretty. Did you sew it up all by yourself?"

"Listen, Polly Kemp, just because I can sew better than . . ." Then a strange expression appeared on Olivia's face. "What . . . what did you say?"

"I said I liked your dress. You matched the

pattern at the seams just right. There's not a lot of people who can do that."

"Why . . . why this old thing?" Olivia spread the skirt for Polly's inspection. "Shucks, it didn't take long to stitch it together. It was real nice of you to admire it, though."

Polly walked on, leaving Olivia shaking her head in puzzlement. Those were the first kind words Olivia had ever heard Polly say. What could have gotten into her, anyway?

Even Charlie Peabody and Alfred Dawes couldn't get Polly's goat. They'd taken over the swings again and weren't about to let somebody else have a chance.

"I'll bet you'd like to swing right now, Polly," sneered Alfred as he swooped down toward her. "But Charlie and me ain't moving for you nor nobody else."

"Fair's fair, Alfred," Polly told him. "You were here first, so I reckon you can swing as long as you like." And she continued on toward the see-saw, leaving two very surprised boys behind her.

Polly made it a point to say something nice to each of the students in Miss Morasco's class that morning, and by noon the whole room was abuzz, all the boys and girls wondering what had come over Polly Kemp. On the playground at noon, Addy Cardiff and Karen Shay asked Polly to join their game of jacks. And Janice Proctor wondered if Polly'd help her learn long division.

Only Agatha Benthorn and Eunice Ingersoll kept their distance. All that day they waited for the croaking to start.

But it never did.

As Polly walked home with the Wickstaff twins after school, it came to her mind that never in her life had she had such a wonderful day. But she couldn't help wondering whether she'd be able to keep her tongue in check at Agatha's house tomorrow.

The next morning Polly got up early and spent a long time getting herself ready before coming downstairs. "Why, Polly," her mother said as she sat down at the table, "you're all dressed up in your Sunday best. Are you sure you want to wear that to school?"

"It's not just for school, Mother," Polly replied. "Miss Agatha Benthorn invited me to her house today for a party." She made a little curtsy.

"Oh? Is the whole class going?"

"No. Just me and Eunice Ingersoll."

"Hmmph!" snorted Mrs. Kemp. She had her own opinions about Agatha and Eunice.

That morning at school, Eunice and Agatha sought Polly out, first thing. "We hope you haven't forgotten our invitation," said Agatha.

"No, I'll be there." But Polly was thinking about how Agatha had said "our invitation." Like she and Eunice were Siamese twins or something, and one of 'em couldn't do anything without the other.

Twice that morning and once more in the afternoon, Polly caught the two with their heads together, pointing at her when they thought she wasn't looking and hee-heeing like a pair of hyenas.

After school the three of 'em bought the little cookies at Stew Meat's store. Then off they went to the Benthorn house.

Mrs. Benthorn, who had a face that put Polly in mind of a Holstein cow, met them at the door. The woman looked down at Polly the way she might examine a fly that had lit in her dish of ice cream.

"Why . . . why Polly Kemp," she said, and her lips pursed distastefully, as if she'd bit into a green persimmon. "I didn't expect you to want to come here after . . . after . . ."

Polly wanted to say something about it being bad manners to treat a guest like something the cat dragged in. But she swallowed her pride, and her face was all innocence as she answered Mrs. Benthorn.

"Ma'am, I know I tore Agatha's dress, and it was a mean and spiteful thing to do, and I apologize for it. I hope I haven't put you to too much trouble on account of it. If there's anything I can do to make good, I'm in your debt."

It was a pretty little speech, and Mrs. Benthorn listened to it dumbfounded. She'd expected something far different from the sharp-tongued Polly Kemp. "No . . . no, Polly," she said with some confusion. "It's quite all right. A few minutes with a needle and thread, and it was all mended. Come in. Come in, please."

Polly stepped into the house. Behind her she could hear Agatha and Eunice whispering.

"I never saw Polly act so nice and polite." Agatha sounded a bit worried.

"What could have come over her?" added Eunice.

They went into the kitchen, and the three girls

took seats at the big table. Mrs. Benthorn put the kettle on to boil and then set the cookies on a plate.

Soon the tea was ready. Polly took a sip. It was boiling hot. She rubbed at her mouth.

"Don't you like the tea, Polly?" Agatha simpered. "It's called oolong, and it comes all the way from China. It's fearfully expensive."

"It's just fine," Polly replied. "It's a lot like the kind my mother makes. Only hers is stronger."

"Oh, my dear girl!" said Agatha. "Surely you can't compare your mother's tea with this costly type. But then, perhaps only a real lady knows how to savor not only the delicate aroma but the exquisite taste. Wouldn't you agree, Eunice, dear?"

Polly managed a thin smile. "I'm sure you're right, Agatha," she said. "I haven't had much practice at being a real lady. But I'm hoping you two can teach me how to do it."

Agatha and Eunice looked at one another in consternation. The whole purpose of inviting Polly was to get her riled, so she'd look like a fool and they could laugh at her. With luck she'd even start *jug-a-rum*ing, the way she did in school. But Polly was being all cool and calm and polite. Agatha decided to try again.

"I love your new dress, Eunice dear," she said grandly. "All that lace—it's quite the style this year. Of course some people have no sense of style at all." And here she stared straight at Polly.

It was like water rolling off a duck's back. "I would so like to be stylish," Polly said. "But my mother makes my clothes, and she's too busy to keep up with the latest fashions. But you do look just beautiful, Eunice."

Neither girl knew what to say. Agatha couldn't criticize Polly's remark without insulting Eunice. And Eunice rather enjoyed the compliment.

"What do you usually do after school, Polly?" Agatha asked. Then she winked her eye at Eunice.

"I usually play down by Spider Crick," Polly replied. "With the Wickstaffs. There's a little pool that's filled with tadpoles every spring. As the days go by, you can see legs start growing out of 'em. And then they turn into frogs. I like watching 'em change."

Agatha made a face. "Ugh! Tadpoles and frogs are horrid things!"

"And so are Leland and Lenora Wickstaff," Eunice added.

"Well, there are flowers along the crick, too. There's jack-in-the-pulpit and Queen Anne's lace and—"

"We have our flowers sent in from a florist," said Eunice with a toss of her head.

"Uh-huh." Polly fought back the urge to say what was on her mind. "And what do you two do? After you've had your tea and cookies, I mean?"

"We do needlepoint," said Agatha.

"And we practice our languages," said Eunice. "I can speak French rather well."

"And we look at the magazines to see what the latest fashions will be."

"And we take our piano lessons."

"And we do all the things that really well-bred girls should do," Agatha concluded.

"That's just fine . . . real fine," replied Polly. "But don't you ever like to get out and do other things, too?"

Agatha and Eunice looked at one another in surprise. "Other things? Like what?"

"Well. . ." Polly had to think about this. "Why, just last month, Lenora Wickstaff learned . . .

taught . . . me how to tickle up a trout. Have either of you tried to do that?"

Eunice looked shocked. "Tickle a trout?"

"Sure. It's real easy. You lie down at the edge of the water, right where some big trout is hiding. You get right down on your belly."

Both girls wrinkled their noses at the word *belly*.

"Then you reach your hand in the water real slow. You move it just a little at a time until you can feel the fish finning itself right there in the palm of your hand. Then, *WHOOSH!* You grab that trout fast and toss him on the bank, and it's fish for dinner."

"How awful!" moaned Agatha.

"How gross!" groaned Eunice.

"I think it's fun," said Polly. "And Leland has promised to show me how he throws a baseball so it curves right in midair. Now that's something to know."

"A real lady doesn't catch fish," said Agatha positively.

"And a real lady doesn't play . . . baseball." Eunice said the word as if the game were some kind of a disease.

Polly just stared at those two girls as if she

was seeing 'em for the first time. She recalled the months and years when she'd have given anything to get an invitation to Agatha's house. Now here she was, and it wasn't at all the pleasant thing she'd expected. It was—it was boring, that's what it was.

All that time wasted. Time when she could have been making lots of real friends and not trying to cozy up to these two frilly, doll-like creatures who wanted no part of her. Olivia Heidecker now—she'd be a friend if Polly didn't scare her off half the time with her sharp tongue. And Janice Proctor, who'd enjoy seeing the fairy ring of toadstools in the woods, and Karen Shay, who could shoot a slingshot straighter'n any boy, and even Charlie Peabody and Alfred Dawes, if she'd give 'em half a chance.

Suddenly Polly wanted to go home or be down by the crick or walking through town or almost anywhere except sitting at a table in the Benthorn kitchen with two priggish girls who thought they were being real ladies when they were really the world's worst snobs.

Polly got to her feet. "I think I'll be leaving now," she said.

"But you can't go!" cried Agatha. "Not until we . . ."

"I can go whenever I want to. The time was, Agatha, when I'd have crawled to this house on hands and knees if I thought you'd invite me inside. But that time is over. I'm my own person now. So I bid you . . . you 'ladies' . . . good-bye."

With that, Polly marched to the front door, where Mrs. Benthorn was standing.

"Good-bye, Polly," she said. "Please come again."

"I do thank you for your hospitality, ma'am. But I don't think I'll be coming back."

"But why not? Didn't you have a good time today?"

"It was . . . interesting. I guess both Agatha and Eunice consider themselves to be real proper ladies. But I must say, Miz Benthorn, I hope I never get to be that kind of a lady."

Before the woman could reply, Polly was out the door.

She ran and ran until she was deep in the woods beyond Spider Crick. Then she looked around until she spotted a big hollow tree. She put her mouth to the opening in its side and began yelling as loud as she could.

"Agatha Benthorn! Eunice Ingersoll! You two ain't got the brains you was born with. There is a whole world out here just waiting to be looked at and used, and all the two of you want to do is look at pictures in magazines and drink tea and eat little cookies. Ladies? You two ain't ladies. You are poor wretched things, and the lowliest animal in the woods has got more life in it than you'll ever have. You are the . . .

"JUG-A-RUM!"

So now she was stuck for a spell, only able to croak like a frog. In spite of that, Polly felt happier than she had in a long time. She threw a stone into Spider Crick just for the pleasure of hearing it *plonk* into the water. Then she climbed high up in a willow tree and looked off toward the Benthorn house in the distance. Agatha and Eunice were in the front yard. To Polly, they looked about the size of a pair of ants.

I don't need those two anymore, Polly thought. I'm free! From her high perch she shouted with joy.

"JUG-A-RUM! JUG-A-RUM! JUG-A-RUM!"

After supper, though, Polly didn't feel quite so happy. Her ma had gone into town for some thread, for the store was open late. Polly sat on the front steps with her hands propping up her chin. "Looks like I'll be saying nothing but nice things from now on," she told herself mournfully. "But knowing me, I'll bust out with something blunt and mean at just the wrong time. Oh, what's it going to be like from now on, having people laughing at me when I start sounding like a swamp critter?

"Consarn that ol' Thaddeus Blinn anyway! That fat little warthog should have known better'n to let me have that wish. He's so . . .

"JUG-A-RUM!"

There were answering croaks from several frogs along the crick. Polly was thankful there was nobody else around to hear. She was stuck, good and proper.

One wish—that's all Thaddeus Blinn had given each of those who'd sat in his tent. Polly wondered if the story she'd heard about Rowena Jervis talking to a bunch of trees had anything to do with the wishing.

If there was any way out of the predicament, it'd take somebody smarter'n Polly herself to find it. But where was there anyone with enough Yankee cleverness and common sense to—

Then a little gasp came from Polly's lips. Perhaps there was a way, after all. If only . . .

Quickly Polly got to her feet. She started at a walk, but her feet moved faster and faster, and soon she was running as fast as she could—running toward where the lights of Coven Tree were blinking on in the twilight.

The Tree Man

As soon as her folks brought her home from the Church Social, Rowena Jervis scurried up the stairs to her room. She placed the red-spotted card from Thaddeus Blinn in the ebony box on the table by her bed and looked at the big calendar on the wall.

The following day—Sunday—was circled in red. Right across the number Rowena had printed a name in big block letters:

HENRY PIPER

"Henry's coming," she sighed to herself. She heard the back door slam downstairs as her pa went out to the barn to see to the livestock. There was a buzz of voices in the kitchen. Sam Waxman, the hired boy, was due to clean up the cellar, and Mrs. Jervis wanted to be sure he did the job right.

Rowena was annoyed. She wanted to talk to her mother alone, not with Sam around. She'd put the thing off as long as she could. If the idea she had in mind was going to work out, she had to see Mama about it right now. Tomorrow would be too late.

She went downstairs, resisting the urge to slide down the banister. That was for children. At fifteen, one had to be more dignified.

Her mother and Sam were seated at the kitchen table. Mrs. Jervis mumbled something to Sam. "Yes'm," he replied, and his thick shock of red hair bobbed about as he nodded his head.

Tall and gangly, Sam seemed to be mostly arms and legs, stuck somehow onto his long stick of a body. But he could do a man's work around the farm. He took his meals with the Jervises and lived in a little room out in the barn.

Rowena wasn't at all fond of Sam. Sam was seventeen and had a way of speaking his mind that she found annoying and sometimes downright rude. Sam was just a bumpkin—so unlike Henry Piper.

"Mama?" she said softly.

"Yes, Rowena?" her mother said. "What is it?"

Sam got to his feet. "I'd best be going out and

help Mr. Jervis in the barn," he said, "so's you two can talk alone."

"Sam Waxman, you stay put," replied Mrs. Jervis firmly. "Clifton said he could do without you for two days while you cleaned the cellar. And I mean to have it done right this time. Anything Rowena's got to tell me won't take long. Now what is it, girl?"

"Well, I . . ." she began. "Mama, Henry Piper will be coming to town tomorrow."

Mrs. Jervis sighed deeply. "I suppose so," she said. "Twice a year, just like clockwork, the Neverfail Farm Implement Company sends that Henry Piper around with his catalog. And your father ends up with more seeders and cultivators and hay forks than he could use around here in a month of Sundays."

"Mother," said Rowena, "Henry would never sell anybody something they didn't need."

"No? Well, you just watch him at his peddling sometime. Flirting with the farm wives and grown daughters, and chucking the babies under their chins. Talking about the far places he's been to and the things he's seen. And all to sell his tools and machinery. I tell you, Henry Piper could charm the socks off a snake. Well, he'll only be here for three days, and I give thanks for that blessing."

"Mama, don't talk so! Henry's just so sophisticated and worldly that it takes a very special kind of person to appreciate him."

Mrs. Jervis scowled at her daughter. "Rowena, you sound almost like you think you're in love with that boy. You're far too young to be even considering such nonsense."

"I'm fifteen, Mama. In only seven more months I'll be sixteen. And I . . . I . . . ."

"Oh, get on with it, Rowena. What was it you wanted to ask me?"

"Well . . . you know Henry always stays at Miz Ballentine's rooming house when he's in town."

"Yes. Where else would he put up?"

"I . . . I was wondering whether he might stay here this time."

Sam let out a snort that a horse would have been proud of. Then he started chuckling behind his hand.

"Sam Waxman, you stop that this instant!" Rowena put her hands on her hips, and her eyes glittered angrily.

"Rowena, you *have* got a thing for that fella, ain't you?" said Sam.

"No, I don't—"

"Yes, you do too. Remember Sunday dinner last fall when he came by? Maybe you didn't think I noticed the two of you holding hands under the tablecloth. And them things he was telling you!"

Sam tried to copy Henry Piper's manner of speaking. "Oh, St. Louis and Boston are fun," he mimicked. "But New York City! Now there's a place where everything is going on at once."

Sam took Rowena's hand. "Rowena," he crooned in a mocking whisper, "we'll walk the streets at three in the morning, and it'll be just like noon, with lights all over the place. Just imagine you in your best dress, sashaying down Broadway on my arm, the two of us looking up at buildings five times as tall as the highest pine in Coven Tree. Then eating in fine restaurants where we'll be served any kind of food you can imagine. Oh, Rowena! My dear one!"

Sam kissed Rowena's hand with a loud smack. She jerked her hand away quickly. The words had sounded so lovely when Henry had said them. And here was Sam, making fun of the whole thing.

"Sam Waxman, you stop it at once!" she

snapped. "I'll have no more of this."

"And I'll have no more talk of Henry Piper's being in this house for three days making calf eyes at you, Rowena," said her mother.

"With all that walking around the city at night, how does Henry manage to get any sleep?" Sam went on.

"If you say one more word, Sam, I'll—"

"Have done, the both of you!" ordered Mrs. Jervis. "Henry's not staying here, and that's flat."

Rowena flounced out of the kitchen and back upstairs to her own room. It just wasn't fair, she thought, flinging herself onto the bed. Bad enough Henry's coming to Coven Tree only twice a year. The least Mama and Daddy could do was let him stay here where she could see him as often as she liked.

Rowena lay on her stomach, imagining how grand it would be if Henry'd settle in Coven Tree. Then she could see him every day. She closed her eyes and pictured him, all fine and neat in his striped suit, with his black hair slicked down.

Then the picture changed. It wasn't Henry she saw in her mind's eye anymore.

It was Thaddeus Blinn.

I can give you whatever you ask for, Blinn's

---

sign had said. Rowena knew what she wanted. She wanted to see Henry a lot more often than a few days twice a year.

She opened her eyes. There, just inches from her face, on the bedside table, was the ebony box. She opened it and took out the red-spotted card. Then she got up, went to the closet, and put the card in the pocket of her best dress.

"We will see what we will see," she said to herself, "as soon as Henry gets here."

The next day, after church, Rowena was out in front gathering some flowers when she heard a shout from the road.

"Hello, the Jervises! Is anyone about?"

Henry Piper! With a glad little cry, Rowena ran toward the gate, calling his name. "Oh, I . . . I'm so glad you've come," she said.

"I couldn't stay away, lovely lady," replied Henry with a deep bow. "I came here first thing, as soon as I got off the train."

Rowena thought she might faint from pure joy. Then she heard a voice behind her.

"You came here first thing, huh? Then how come you ain't got no bags with you except that little case with your catalog and order slips in

it? Naw, you got yourself fixed in at Miz Ballentine's first. Got all freshened up. Your hair's still
wet."

Ohh, that Sam! Rowena could have killed him!

"Sam Waxman, ain't you got anything better
to do than stand gawking while two old friends
get reacquainted?"

"Yep. Reckon I do." Sam looked Henry up and
down. "It won't do for me to stand here talking.
That's Henry's department—talking." And off he
walked toward the barn.

"Never mind Sam," Rowena said sweetly.
"You come inside, Henry. Perhaps you can stay
for dinner."

"Perhaps I can, my dear. I have a whole new
line of machinery I want to talk to your father
about."

Rowena pouted prettily.

"And later, maybe you and I can have a few
words together—alone." When Henry said
"alone" that way, Rowena's innards felt like they
were filled with butterflies.

Henry stayed the whole day. He spent most
of the afternoon in the front parlor with Mr. Jervis, talking about machinery. It wasn't until that
evening that Rowena got Henry to herself. They

sat on the big back porch, watching the last of the sunset.

Rowena was of two minds about Henry. She was, of course, delighted to have him there. But she was already thinking ahead to the time two days hence when he'd be leaving Coven Tree.

"After tomorrow I have some time off from school," she said hopefully. "And on Tuesday, Susannah Haskill is giving a party. I thought perhaps you could . . . I mean, we could . . ."

But Henry just laughed. "Silly goose," he replied, tweaking her nose. "What would the Neverfail Farm Implement Company think if they found their best salesman going off to parties instead of tending to business?"

Rowena sighed. She was sure Henry liked her. If only he'd come right out and *say* so.

"Almost dark," Henry said. "I'd best be getting back to Miz Ballentine's."

"Can't you stay just a little longer?" Rowena pleaded.

"I expect your pa would like you inside and me gone. I'll just cut across the backyard. Until tomorrow, Rowena."

And without waiting for a reply, he stepped off the porch.

Two more days, and then Henry'd be gone again for another six months. Rowena couldn't bear the thought of it. From the pocket of her best dress she took out the card she'd placed there yesterday. She pressed her thumb firmly against the red spot and made her wish:

"I wish . . . I wish Henry Piper would put down roots here in Coven Tree and never leave again!"

The spot on the card suddenly felt warm against her thumb.

Henry had disappeared into the darkness. In the still night air Rowena heard a rustling sound. It was accompanied by grunts and groans and heavy breathing, and it seemed to be coming from the thick grove of trees back where the lawn ended and the fields began. At first Rowena thought it might be some wild critter who'd gotten tangled with a tree limb.

But then she heard the voice. It was little more than a whisper: "Consarn it! Rowena, come help me!"

Rowena seized a lantern from the porch, lit it, and held it in front of her as she crossed the backyard to the grove of trees. They grew in a circle, and their tangled branches made it hard for her to enter. Finally she forced her way in and held the lantern high.

There stood Henry Piper, mumbling angry words. He was bent over, and at first Rowena thought he was pulling up his sock. Then she saw it was the ankle itself he was yanking up on.

"Henry?" Rowena gasped. "What are you doing, lurking about here? I thought you'd be half-way back to Miz Ballentine's by now."

"Keep your voice down, Rowena. I . . . I don't want anybody else to come out here and find me in this fix."

"Fix? What fix, Henry?"

"It's my feet. They seem to be stuck to the ground. And I can't move either of 'em, no matter how hard I try."

"**H**enry, are you spoofing me?"

But Henry wasn't playing any joke. He stood in the center of the circle of trees with both feet planted firmly together on the earth. From the look on his face, Rowena could see he was plain, deep-down scared!

"I'm stuck, I tell you," he said in a quavering voice. "It's like I was glued to the earth. You'd better get me loose right quick, Rowena Jervis."

Rowena knelt and looked carefully at Henry's feet and ankles. They didn't seem to be caught in any trap. She grasped his right leg and yanked up hard. Nothing happened.

"I'll get Daddy," she said. "Maybe he—"

"You'll do nothing of the kind," Henry replied. "If word of this gets out, I'll be a laughingstock in the whole county. I'll be finished as a sales-man. You just keep your mouth shut and get me loose. Try wrapping your arms about me and lifting."

Rowena got behind Henry and threw her arms about him. For months she'd yearned to have her arms around Henry Piper. But not when something like this was happening.

She heaved upward. For all the good it did, she might as well have been trying to haul a full-grown tree out of the ground.

"It . . . it isn't working, Henry."

"Then do something else," he ordered.

"Rowena!" It was Mr. Jervis, calling from the back porch.

"Yes, Daddy?"

"Are you out there with Henry Piper? That young jackanapes never did say good-bye."

Rowena was about to say yes when she saw Henry scowling at her. "No, Daddy!" she called back. "I'm alone. I'll be right in."

"Don't you dare let on to your father that I'm out here," Henry whispered through clenched teeth. "I never felt so foolish in my life."

"I won't tell. But I must go inside. Can I do

something to make you more comfortable, Henry?"

"I'm chilly. I need a coat or something."

"I'll just go in the house and . . ."

"No! Your pa will get to wondering. Get something from the barn."

The only thing Rowena could find was an old horse blanket. She wrapped it around Henry. "That should keep you warm," she said. "Tomorrow I'll be out first thing and bring you breakfast. Or maybe you'll get free in the meantime."

Henry sniffed at the blanket and wrinkled his nose. "Phoo!" he exclaimed. "This old thing stinks of hay and horse sweat. Haven't you got anything cleaner?"

Rowena glared at him. "You said you didn't want me to go into the house, Henry."

"Then I suppose it'll have to do."

Rowena ran off toward the house, while Henry clutched the smelly blanket close about him and tried to stop the chattering of his teeth.

Rowena didn't sleep much that night. She was too jittery and upset—and a little scared—by what had happened. Henry Piper, stuck to the ground—had ever there been such a thing before? By morning she was so logy and puff eyed that her mother wondered if she was sick.

"No, Mama. Just a bit tired."

As soon as she could, Rowena sneaked out to the grove of trees with a doughnut from the breakfast table. Henry stood there, shivering in the blanket.

"I brought you this, Henry," said Rowena.

"A doughnut," he sneered. "If it wasn't for coming to see you, I'd be down at Miz Ballentine's right now, eating ham and eggs. All you've got is an old doughnut. Well, I don't need it."

"You've got to eat, Henry."

"I feel like I've been eating all night. Only the food came up from my feet instead of down from my mouth. What in tarnation has happened to me, Rowena?"

"Henry, I really think I should tell somebody—"

"You just keep that mouth of yours shut, young lady!"

"Henry Piper, you never in your life talked to me like that before," said Rowena. "But . . . well don't start worrying. We'll get you free. Let me find you something to sit on."

"I've got every right to worry," Henry replied.

"And as for sitting, I can't do it. My knees won't bend. I'm stiff from the waist down. Never mind a chair. Just get rid of this smelly blanket."

"All right, Henry. But then I have to go to school. I'll come back, soon as I can."

"You'd better," said Henry sternly. "I'm stuck on your property, so you have to look after me until I get loose."

Rowena walked out of the grove of trees. Suddenly she turned and stuck out her tongue at the spot where Henry was standing.

The school day passed almost like a dream—or a nightmare. Afterward Rowena ran all the way home, hoping to slip in the back door without anybody seeing her. But Mama was in the kitchen.

"Sit down, Rowena," said Mrs. Jervis. "I want to talk to you."

Rowena put a hand to her lips. Had Mama discovered . . . ?

"Did you pass the grade school on your way home?" Mama asked.

Rowena shook her head. "I took the short cut. Why?"

"Clara Fessengill came by today, and she said

Polly Kemp was croaking like a frog in school. I thought you might have heard—"

"Oh, Mama, you know Polly. She'd do anything to get attention."

"No, Clara said it was like Polly couldn't help herself. As if croaking had taken the place of talking."

"Clara Fessengill's an old gossip . . ." Rowena began. Then she suddenly closed her mouth, and a little shiver ran up her spine.

"Excuse me, Mama." Rowena darted through the back door and out of her mother's sight. Polly Kemp, acting strangely—Polly who'd sat right next to her in Thaddeus Blinn's tent. What was going on? . . .

In the midst of the circle of trees she found Henry just as she'd left him. No, not quite the same. "I seem to be losing my voice, too," he told her in a harsh whisper. "You've got to get me loose."

"But how, Henry?"

"Maybe you can pry me free. Get that long branch there."

Rowena got the branch.

"Now bring it over here."

Rowena did as she was told.

93

"Can't you move any faster, Rowena?" Henry wheezed. "Now slide the end of it under my foot. No, you ninny, not that end! The other one. Goldurn you, Rowena, stop being so infernally dumb!"

Could this be the same Henry Piper she'd thought was so marvelous only yesterday? "I'm doing the best I can," she said.

"Well, your best isn't all that good. Now get a piece of wood—not that one, dad-blast it, *that* one! Stick it underneath the pole. Take it easy there. It feels like you're tickling my foot."

Rowena was too upset by all the orders Henry was spouting at her to wonder how he could feel tickling right through the sole of his shoe. "Now push down on the pole," Henry went on. "Push harder, you silly . . . oww! What are you trying to do, cripple me?"

"You told me to pry, Henry. I'm prying. I can't keep things straight when you're giving me all those orders at the same time."

"You're just like all the rest. Not enough sense to boil water."

All the rest? All *what* rest? Rowena wondered. But before she could ask Henry, she heard another voice behind her.

"Rowena, I thought I seen you in here, and . . . what the dickens!"

Sam! With a guilty start Rowena turned to face him.

Sam scowled at Rowena. "Have you and Henry been sneaking—"

"No! It's not like that at all." Suddenly it was important to Rowena that Sam understand what she and Henry were doing in the grove. "Henry's feet got stuck to the ground somehow, and—"

"Yeah, I'll bet they did," muttered Sam. "Well, I'll pry him loose in a hurry."

Sam put his whole weight on the lever. Henry's cries of pain were oddly muffled, as if they came from a distant valley.

"Hush up, Henry," said Sam. "D'you want to get loose or not?"

Finally Sam had to give up. "I guess you're right, Rowena," he said. "Henry's stuck fast. It's eerie. I never saw the like before. . . . Do your folks know about this?"

"No, and you ain't gonna tell 'em, either," said Henry.

"Don't you be giving me orders, Henry," Sam said. "Now, if we're going to get you loose, we first have to see what's holding you down."

Sam took out his jackknife and knelt at Henry's feet.

"Sam, you be careful," Henry said. "It's scary enough, just being stuck here. I don't want to get cut, too."

"Hmmm. That's odd," said Sam.

"What's odd?" asked Henry.

"Your shoes. Leather's all cracked. It looks for all the world like bark on a tree. And the bark goes clear up to your ankles. Well, I'll soon cut you loose."

Sam thrust the knife blade under Henry's right shoe.

"Aaarrghhh!" Henry's scream wasn't very loud, sounding like he had a blanket wrapped about his head. But Rowena gasped in alarm.

"You hurt me, Sam," Henry whimpered. "You cut my foot with your knife."

Sam looked up. "Henry, I swear I was digging way down below the sole of your shoe and—"

"Sam, look at that!" cried Rowena, pointing. "That red stuff on the blade of your knife. It looks like blood."

"Blood!" shrieked Henry as loud as he could. "My blood!"

"But how could . . . ?" Sam began. Then he started digging below Henry's shoes with his fingers. It was slow going, but finally the earth beneath Henry's right heel had been scraped away.

"Look there, Rowena," said Sam. From the bottom of Henry's foot were growing . . .

"Roots?" Rowena asked, astonished.

"Roots," Sam replied.

"You mean Henry is rooted to the ground like a . . . a *tree*?"

"It seems so. And if we cut those roots, it'd be like stabbing a knife into Henry's body. It might even kill him."

"Don't do it, then!" moaned Henry. "I don't want to die!"

"But what could have caused Henry to grow roots and . . . ?" Rowena began. Then she started trembling and shaking all over as she finally understood the thing she'd done to Henry Piper.

Roots! Rowena had said the word before, just a short time ago. Last night on the porch—she'd pressed her thumb onto the spot on the wish card and wished . . . wished that . . .

. . . *Henry Piper would put down roots here in Coven Tree and never leave again!*

"Oh, Sam!" Rowena cried as tears filled her eyes. "Ooohh, Saaam!"

"And . . . and then I wished on the card that Henry'd put down roots here in Coven Tree. But all I meant was for him to stay put and not be a traveling man anymore. Instead he's got real roots, and he's *stuck*!"

Rowena barely finished telling Sam and Henry about Thaddeus Blinn's magic before she burst into bitter tears. "Oh, Sam, what am I going to do?"

But neither Sam nor Henry was listening. Sam was looking at Henry like he was seeing a dragon or an ogre or some other mystical beast. And Henry was staring with fear and trembling at his own bark-covered ankles.

"Henry did put down roots. Real ones, just like you asked for," said the awestruck Sam.

"Magic—that's the only thing that could have done this."

"Just like Polly Kemp's croaking," said Rowena. "She got one of the cards too, and it must be the same magic that—"

"Never mind Polly Kemp." Henry's voice was like the rustle of wind through leafy branches. "What about *me*? I'm the one who's stuck here. And it's getting worse all the time. Bark's creeping up my legs. I'm getting stiffer and stiffer. Food seems to be coming up to me from the roots growing out of my feet. And now it's getting hard for me to talk."

"Sam," Rowena moaned. "He's turning into a . . . a . . ."

"A tree," said Sam.

"Rowena, do something!" Henry yelled hoarsely.

"Calm down, Henry," said Sam. "None of us have had much experience with magic. It may take a bit of time to figure something out."

"But I haven't got time," Henry said. "I'm changing . . . changing. . . ."

"Maybe I should go looking for Thaddeus Blinn," said Rowena. "Maybe he'd come back and revoke the wish. He's only been gone two days. He can't have gotten far."

"No," said Sam with a shake of his head. "A human couldn't go far. But Blinn seems to be a creature of magic. He could be on the far side of the moon by now."

"Then maybe Daddy or Mama could think of something."

"Most likely you'd just start 'em worrying, and they'd spread word about Henry all over town," Sam replied. "Then we'd have people milling around out here and either laughing at Henry or else giving advice that isn't worth a hill of beans. I say we keep this to ourselves. Rowena, you were the one who took the card from Thaddeus Blinn, and you made the wish on it. So you'll have to find a way to release Henry from the spell. Nobody else can do it for you."

"And hurry!" Henry added.

"But I can't think of anything," said Rowena.

"Then the least we can do is make Henry comfortable until you come up with an idea," said Sam. "Maybe if we pulled up the weeds around his feet, it'd help." Sam walked in a circle about

Henry. Then he bent down and picked up a leather case from a clump of weeds. "What's this?"

"That's what I keep my catalog and order blanks in," Henry said. "Don't you go opening that, Sam Waxman."

"All right, Henry. I'll just put it in the barn where it won't get wet. Rowena, you start pulling those weeds."

As Sam left the clearing, Rowena began yanking at the weeds. Henry started giving orders like a slave driver. "Don't get too close to my feet, Rowena. . . . Take bigger handfuls, Rowena. . . . Pile 'em over there, Rowena. . . . There's one you missed, Rowena. . . ."

"Henry Piper, you shut your face!" Rowena snapped suddenly. "I'm doing the best I can. Don't you think I feel bad enough without you jawing at me all the time?"

"You're to blame for me—"

"I didn't mean for things to turn out this way. Oh, Henry, whatever happened to all the nice things you used to tell me about how pretty I was and all them fine places you visited? If I'm at all special to you, you shouldn't be carrying on this way, even if your feet are stuck to the ground."

"Special? That's a laugh."

"But the way you used to talk, I *had* to be special, Henry."

"Listen, Rowena Jervis. I'd have said you were Cleopatra or the Queen of Sheba if that's what I had to do. Anything so you'd tell your papa how nice I was and I could sell him more machinery."

"Henry, you . . . you can't mean that!"

"I do mean it! Fall in love with you? D'you think I'm an idiot? You're nothing but a silly, lovesick goose."

"And you are a worm, Henry Piper!" Rowena cried out. "If I'd known for a second you didn't mean all those fine things you said, I'd . . . I'd . . ."

"You'd never have made that stupid wish. And I'd be free instead of stuck here talking to you."

"I'll get you free somehow," said Rowena through clenched teeth. "If only to see you getting aboard the train and headed out of town. Forever!"

"But until I get loose, you've got to care for me, Rowena. You've got to do anything I want."

"But only until I find a way to remove the spell. After that—well, you'd just better watch out, Henry Piper!"

Sam walked back into the clearing. He carried a paper sack, a bucket of water, and a small spade. He took a handful of powder from the bag and sprinkled it around Henry's feet.

"This is stuff to make trees grow," he said.

Sam worked the ground up with the spade. Finally he poured the water over Henry's shoes.

"Ohhh," Henry moaned with contentment. "That feels real good, Sam. See, Rowena? Sam knows how to treat me properly."

"Sam, did you hear what Henry was saying? He didn't mean a single one of all those fine things he used to tell me."

"I never figured he did," Sam replied. "But if I'd said so, you wouldn't have listened. You had to learn for yourself. Here's something else to keep in mind now that you know what Henry's really like. The sooner you think of a way to wish the spell off him, the sooner he'll be out of your life for good. So put your whole mind to it, Rowena. Me, I've got farm work to do. I'll leave you two alone."

Rowena stayed with her unwelcome guest until late that evening, taking only time for supper. In spite of Sam's confidence that she'd find a way to free Henry, she kept thinking about how he might never get loose. She'd have to spend the rest of her life caring for that . . . that ignoramus who'd become rooted in her backyard. Two days ago she'd wanted more than anything for Henry to remain in Coven Tree. Now she couldn't stand the sight of him.

The next morning at breakfast, Rowena's mother had a question. "What's so all-fired interesting about that clump of trees out in back?" she asked. "You're spending a lot of time there, child."

"It's a fine place to study, Mama," she said. "This week we have to get ready for tests at school."

"Just don't get studying so hard you forget about the Haskills' party tonight. Everybody in your class will be there."

The party! With all the trouble Henry'd given her, Rowena had forgotten all about it. But how could she go? Henry needed caring for, and she had to . . .

"I just wish he'd dry up and blow away!" she cried. Then Rowena stomped out of the kitchen, leaving her mother to wonder what in tarnation she was talking about.

Rowena just had to talk to somebody. She found Sam in the barn and poured out to him her disappointment at missing the Haskills' party.

Much to her surprise, Sam seemed to understand. "You go along to your party," he told her. "I'll stay with Henry this evening. Though I warn you, Rowena, if he gets to complaining too much, I intend to stuff a rag in his mouth and stomp it home with my foot."

That evening, the Haskill house was all decorated with Japanese lanterns and paper streamers. Everybody seemed to be having fun—everybody but Rowena. She had on her prettiest dress, and all her friends from school were there, but it was impossible for her to enjoy the party. She still felt guilty about leaving Sam to take her proper place in the grove of trees.

She was sitting in a corner and staring at her shoes when Ruth Higgens and Minnie Baldwin walked by. Minnie was talking a mile a minute, and Rowena heard her mention Adam Fiske. Rowena remembered Adam sitting on the far end of the bench in Thaddeus Blinn's tent. Leaning forward, she cupped her hand behind her ear.

". . . All spraying way up into the air, right there at the corner of Adam's house," Minnie was saying. "Ruth, I don't care what folks say about there being no water on the Fiske farm. My daddy saw it, I tell you."

"Underground springs sometimes do that," Ruth replied.

"Not like this. Daddy says it was . . . was *magic*!"

Magic? Then Adam must have been wishing too, Rowena thought. But water? On that dried-out Fiske farm? If that's what Adam wished for, he was lucky. At least he'd gotten something useful from his wish.

After the party Mr. Haskill took Rowena and several of the others home in his big wagon. "It's all dark at your place," he told Rowena when they reached the Jervis house. "D'you want me to see you to the door?"

"No thanks, I'll be fine." Rowena hopped down

107

from the wagon and made her way across the lawn to the front porch.

She grasped the knob of the front door. Suddenly the old rocking chair at the far end of the porch creaked loudly. "Who's there?" she called, scared stiff.

"Only me—Sam." She heard footsteps coming across the porch, and then he was standing beside her.

"I reckon you'd better take a look at Henry," Sam said. "It's a lot worse than we ever figured on. It's happening faster now."

"What's worse?" she asked as they walked through the darkness toward the grove of trees. "What's happening faster?"

"You'll see."

Once inside the grove, Sam lit the lantern and held it up. There was Henry. But it was a Henry that Rowena hardly recognized.

The rough bark that had been around his ankles now covered his whole body, clear up to the chin. But that wasn't all. Now his arms were thrust stiffly upward and outward, for all the world like gnarled limbs of wood. As Sam held the lantern closer, Rowena was horrified.

"Sam," she said in a scared whisper, "he's almost like a real tree!"

Only Henry's face showed that the thing growing there was—or had once been—human. And even that was twisted into a shape like weatherworn wood. The expression on it was one of pure horror. The lips moved, but only a soft sighing came from them.

Rowena leaned closer. There was the merest whisper of breath from the open mouth. There were words, too—words that made Rowena shiver in the warm spring night.

"Help me! Help me!"

By Wednesday after-
noon, everything that was human in Henry
Piper had disappeared. All that was left was tree.

Oh, a person looking close at the big knob near
the top of the trunk might make out two eyes
and a mouth amid the grain of the wood. But
for all intents and purposes, Henry was just a
runty sycamore standing in the midst of the
grove of trees.

Rowena was at her wits' end. Somehow she
had to get Henry back to being human. She
turned the problem over in her mind for hours
on end without coming up with a single idea
of how to go about it. She had to keep Pa and
Ma from finding out, too. They'd never understand, especially since Henry didn't look any-

thing like Henry anymore. They'd probably think she'd gone soft in the head.

Rowena knew she couldn't have stood it without Sam's being there to help. That night she lay in her bed, imagining how things might have been if it had been Sam who'd changed into a tree and she'd sought help from Henry. She decided Henry'd have been worse than no help at all.

She was sure Sam would have accepted his fate with a dignity that Henry Piper would never know. And Sam wouldn't have become any puny softwood sycamore, either. Sam would have been a mighty oak.

Sam. For three days Rowena'd been so wrapped up in her own problems that she'd never once said a word to him about how grateful she was for . . . for his just being there. Sometimes she'd get so worried about Henry's plight that she'd go all sick inside and want to scream and scream, or else run off somewhere and hide. Then Sam would give her a wink or a nod or a few whispered words, and she'd find the strength to go on. She'd tell Sam in the morning how much that meant to her.

But in the morning, Sam was gone.

"He asked me for some time to go into town," Pa explained. "He didn't say what for."

Sam barely made it back in time for supper, and afterward there were chores to be done. It wasn't until nearly eight o'clock that Rowena found him alone.

"Where have you been all day?" she asked.

"Reading, mostly—in the school library. I got to thinking that if magic can turn a person into a tree, maybe there's a spell of some kind that'll turn him back into a man again."

"Did you find one?" Rowena asked hopefully.

"Nope. Only legends and such. People worshiping trees on account of gods were supposed to be inside, or they were the souls of dead people."

"But nothing about a person changing . . ."

"I did find some old stories," Sam replied, "where folks got changed into plants of different kinds. The closest I could get to Henry's problem was one about a gal called Daphne who got turned into a laurel tree to escape from the god Apollo. But those yarns are more fanciful than real, I expect.

"Still, it can't all be superstition. Anybody

thinking that would have a real eye-opener just by looking into that grove out yonder. Though Henry's so much tree now, probably nobody'd even notice him."

"I'm grateful for what you tried to do, anyway," Rowena told him. "But sooner or later somebody's going to come looking for Henry. What'll I say? 'Knock on the trunk of that sycamore and see if anybody's home'?"

"We've got a few days before anybody comes searching," Sam said. "Y'see, I called the Neverfail Company from Stew Meat's store. I said Henry'd been taken sick. The lady on the phone was ever so nice. She said Henry was only to think about getting better, and somebody else would handle his selling until he was up and about."

"Oh, Sam, I've been such a dunce," said Rowena. "If I hadn't made a fool of myself over Henry, none of this would have happened. But when he talked of all those fine places he'd been to, it was like I was right there with him. New York . . . St. Louis . . . even Paris. I'll never get to any of those cities, Sam. But just talking to somebody who'd been there was . . . was . . ."

"Rowena," said Sam suddenly, "I ain't ever been outside this county. But I've got a few things I want to say to you."

"All right, Sam," she said, looking oddly at him. "But what . . . ?"

"I want you to pretend I'm Henry Piper," Sam told her. "The old Henry, before he changed. Can you do that?"

"It'll be hard," she replied. "But I'll try."

"Rowena, my dear," Sam began, taking her hand. "Let me tell you about London."

"Sam Waxman, London's way across the ocean in England. You haven't ever been near there."

"Come on, Rowena. You never stopped Henry in the middle of a story. I'm supposed to be him, remember?"

"All right, Sam . . . I mean Henry. Go ahead."

"In London is a cathedral called St. Paul's, with a big round dome at the top. I recollect standing on the balcony that runs around the underside of that dome and—"

"Sam, you're being silly."

"Shhh, Rowena. This ain't Sam talking. It's Henry. So I whispered against the dome, and the whisper was heard only by the person way across on the other side. Nobody else heard a sound because the words followed the curve of the dome. Someday, Rowena, you and I will

---

115

stand on opposite sides of that dome, and I'll whisper—"

"This is nonsense, Sam."

"No, it ain't. It's true. And for now, my name's Henry. In China there's a wall clear across the whole country. It's so big you could be on the moon and still see it. And there's islands where bugs build homes higher'n your pa's barn, and people shinny up coconut trees by tying their feet together. If we was to walk along the beach of one of those islands, Rowena, we'd see fish in the water that are every color of the rainbow. Away out in San Francisco they've got trolley cars without motors, and they're pulled by a cable buried in the street and—"

"Sam Waxman, you stop this instant!" cried Rowena. "None of that stuff you told me is real."

"Oh, it's real, right enough."

"How do you know? You've never been to any of those places."

"Nope," said Sam. "I ain't. And neither has Henry Piper!"

"Sam, you don't have to start lying about Henry just so I'll feel better—"

"It's the truth, Rowena. The lady at Neverfail

said Henry has an Aunt Bertha down in Bridge-port, Connecticut, who'd want to know about his being sick. So I called her, too. She told me a few things about Henry that were real interesting."

"What did she tell you?"

"It seems Henry works for the Neverfail Company fifty weeks a year, selling in the state of Maine and a little part of New Hampshire. On his two-week vacation, he stays with Aunt Bertha, painting and fixing her place up to earn a little extra money. So he never had the time to visit all those fancy places he talks about."

"Then how'd he find out so much about them?" asked Rowena in astonishment.

"Same way I did. Wait here a minute. I want to get something from the barn."

Sam returned a few moments later carrying the leather case he'd found at Henry's feet.

"I looked inside," Sam said. "There's more than catalogs and order blanks in here."

He opened the case and pulled out . . .

"Magazines!" Rowena exclaimed.

"Yep. Here's *Travel Topics*, and an old copy of *Our Country in Pictures*. I read in *Travel*

Topics about London and China and all those other places I told you about. The story about New York City is the humdinger. It tells all about the night life and how everything's as bright as day, and all the fine restaurants, and . . ."

"You mean Henry'd just *read* about all those places he said he'd been to? He was never really in any of them?"

"Looks that way, Rowena."

"Why, that no-good, sweet-talking . . . mule!" she sputtered. "To think I mooned about, making calf eyes at him, and all the time he was lying through his teeth. Oh, Sam, I feel so . . . so stupid."

"Don't be too hard on yourself," said Sam. "Henry's paying a high price for his foolishness as it is. I just thought knowing the trick he pulled might make you feel easier, seeing as there doesn't seem to be any way of changing him back right soon."

For a moment Rowena just sat quietly. Then suddenly she pounded her fist hard against the arm of her chair. "No!" she exclaimed. "No! No! No! I'll not have Henry Piper cluttering up that grove of trees for all the years to come and reminding me always of my own foolishness.

118

There's a way out of this fix. There *must* be!"

"But Rowena, you said Thaddeus Blinn only gave you one wish."

"You don't have to remind me, Sam. I remember it like I was sitting on that bench in his tent right now. Him in his white suit and red vest, handing out those red-spotted cards. One to Polly . . . one to me . . . one to . . . to . . ."

Rowena lapsed into silence. For several moments she stared long and hard at Sam.

"I know how," she said finally.

"How? How what?" Sam asked.

"I know how to get Henry Piper back to being a man again," she replied, growing more and more excited. "What time is it?"

"About eight thirty. But how are you going to—"

"No time now for explaining. I'll have to hurry. Come with me, Sam."

Sam shook his head. "Wherever you're off to, Rowena, you must do this thing alone. You got Henry into this fix by yourself, and if you know how, you must free him from the spell the same way."

"Then will you at least wait up for me until I come back?"

———

119

He looked down at her and smiled. It seemed to Rowena that something about Sam had changed. His face wasn't that of a boy anymore, but that of a man. And when he spoke, it was in a man's voice, strong and sure, yet soft and comforting.

"Rowena Jervis, I've already been waiting for you a long time. But until now, you only had eyes for Henry Piper. Yes, Rowena, I'll wait. Take all the time you need. And when you're ready for me, you'll find me waiting still."

Water,
Water,
Everywhere

"**N**o rain for three weeks. Well's gone dry, and the cistern's near empty. Tomorrow after school, you'd best haul the tubs down to Spider Crick and fill 'em up."

Those were the first words Adam Fiske's pa said to him on Sunday morning. They made Adam angry.

Yesterday's Church Social had been fun, and Adam had stayed late. When he'd gotten home, he'd hung his pants in the closet, with the red-spotted card still in the pocket, and gotten right into bed. He had woken on Sunday morning with all the fun still fresh in his mind.

Now Pa had to ruin it all.

"Do I have to?" Adam complained. "Everybody laughs at me when I drive the wagon through town. And filling all those tubs from the crick takes forever. They sure do hold a lot of water."

"Well, doesn't seem like much by the time you get home," Adam's ma put in. "What with drinking and cooking and washing and water for the animals and trying to keep the crops from burning, it's gone in no time. Until it rains, you'll probably be hauling every day, Adam. Get used to it."

"It don't seem fair," Adam grumbled. "This is the only farm in Coven Tree where the well goes dry if it doesn't rain regular every three days. Besides, what would be the harm in getting water from the spring on Mr. Jenks's farm? What he doesn't use just soaks back underground. That way I wouldn't have to go through town and—"

"That's enough, Adam!" Pa snapped. "This is our farm, and we'll run it without asking charity from anybody. We'll take our water from Spider Crick, and you'll haul all that's necessary."

Well, there it was. Pa'd saved for a long time to buy this land, and he'd built the house and barn with his own hands. His stubborn pride refused to allow him to become beholden to any man.

"Oh, cheer up, Adam," Pa went on. "Tomorrow

Uncle Poot will be here. We'll find water yet."

"Uncle Poot?" said Adam. "The dowser man?"

"Yep. He doesn't get down to this end of the valley much, but I asked him special, and he agreed. That forked stick of his never makes a mistake. Dig a well where a dowser man's stick points, and you'll soon strike water."

"Maybe," said Adam doubtfully. He couldn't believe that dowsing really worked. Most likely he'd be hauling water from Spider Crick for the rest of his life.

After breakfast the next morning Adam set out for school. On the way he met Polly Kemp on the road. "Good morning, Polly," he called as he caught up to her. "After today I've got a few days off before final tests start. What do you think of that?"

"JUG-A-RUM!"

Well, if that wasn't just like Polly! Making strange noises instead of giving a civil answer. "You don't have to get sassy with me, Polly Kemp," Adam said crossly.

"JUG-A-RUM!"

She was rude, to be sure. But it did beat all, how much Polly sounded like a real frog. He told her so, hoping she'd be pleased.

"JUG-A-RUM!"

After a final remark, Adam trotted on.

At school he sat right behind Rowena Jervis in science class. Rowena was usually a good student. But not today. Her mind seemed a million miles away. She kept sniffling and sighing and murmuring something about . . . well, "feet stuck" was what it sounded like. But maybe he'd just heard wrong.

When Adam got home from school, he harnessed Hank and Herb, their two horses, to the big flat wagon. He loaded the eight huge iron tubs onto the wagon bed and climbed up to the seat. "Giddap," he ordered with a flick of the reins.

Off they went, with the tubs in back clanking loud enough to drown out the clopping of the horses' hoofs.

At the edge of town the hooting began. "Here comes ol' Adam Fiske with his water-draggin' wagon!" yelled Orville Hopper.

"I guess they're getting mighty thirsty out there!" jeered somebody from inside the firehouse.

He passed Agatha Benthorn and Eunice Ingersoll on their way home from school. The two girls made faces and stuck their noses in the air. Adam about died of embarrassment.

Once through town and down by the crick, Adam pulled the wagon as close to the water as he could get. He took off his shoes and socks, and rolled up his pant legs. Then he took a bucket from under the wagon seat and climbed down to the ground.

He waded into the icy water of the crick and scooped up a bucketful. Then he walked to the wagon, with the sharp stones cutting at his bare feet, and poured the water into one of the tubs. The whole bucketful seemed scarcely to cover the tub's bottom.

Scoop . . . pour . . . scoop . . . pour . . . scoop . . . pour . . . Time after time Adam lifted buckets of water, until his shoulders felt as if they were being pierced by a white-hot iron bar. By the time all the tubs were filled, the sweat was dripping from his chin, and his feet were almost numb from the cold crick water.

Then there was the return trip to make. Again there were jokes and catcalls from the villagers; and then, just as he approached the farm, one wagon wheel hit a rock, jarring the filled tubs.

Water sloshed loudly onto the wagon bed and then poured down into the dirt. Where once the tubs had been full to the top, now they were almost a third empty. One third of Adam's work, soaking into the dry earth.

"Consarn!" he muttered angrily.

Pa was in the front yard, pacing back and forth next to a white-haired little man who was slender as a reed and looked to be a hundred years old. In each palm-up fist, the old man gripped one prong of a forked applewood branch some three feet long. His eyes were glued to the spot where the prongs met and formed a kind of pointer that shook slightly as he walked.

"Stop and give the horses a rest, Adam," said Pa as the wagon rolled up beside him. "Come and meet Uncle Poot."

"Durnedest thing I ever seen," Uncle Poot muttered as Adam climbed down from the wagon. "Seems like there should be water under this land. But I've covered every inch, and the rod didn't twitch once."

Adam looked curiously at the branch in Uncle Poot's hands. "It don't seem possible," Adam said, "to find water under the ground with just an old stick."

"It ain't hard," Uncle Poot replied. "For those of us who have the gift."

"The gift?"

"The dowsing gift, boy. Only one person in a thousand—mebbe *two* thousand—has it, the way I do. Without the gift, a man could tote this stick over the whole state of Maine and never know when there was water right under his feet.

"But you can find the water, huh?"

"Dang tootin' I can! When I walk over an underground stream holding the prongs of my dowsing rod, t'other end of it will twist down and point to water like a fish pole when a trout hits the lure."

"Are you ever wrong?" asked Adam. "Does the stick ever point when there isn't any water?"

"Never," said Uncle Poot. "Why, didn't I dowse Luke Jenks a well right in his backyard after he'd sunk four dry holes looking for water? Ten feet down in the spot I pointed was water enough for him, and the neighbors on either side as well. And Dan'l Pitt had near given up finding water, but I dowsed it for him."

Then the old man shrugged. "But there's got to be water there for me to find it. And there's none under this farm. Sorry, Mr. Fiske."

"It ain't your fault, Uncle Poot," said Pa with a sigh.

The dowser man started to walk off. But Adam had an idea.

"Uncle Poot," he said, "could I have that dowsing rod?"

"This old stick?" Uncle Poot held the branch out to Adam. "Take it and welcome. I can cut me another anytime. But don't expect it to find water for you. The power's not in the dowsing rod, but in the person holding it."

"Maybe I have the dowsing gift, Uncle Poot."

"Mebbe," the dowser man replied doubtfully. "But it ain't likely. The gift's a rare thing."

With that, Uncle Poot shuffled off down the path. Adam grasped the prongs of the branch and slowly walked the length of the yard. The stick bobbed slightly at each step, but never did it twist and point to the ground the way the dowser man had described.

"Face it, Adam," said Pa. "We'll be hauling water until it rains."

At supper that evening, Ma brought up something that had been on her mind for some time. "I'd like to grow flowers outside the kitchen window," she said. "They'd be pleasant to look at."

"Flowers need a heap of water," said Pa. "How 'bout it, Adam? You'd be the one doing the hauling."

At first Adam felt like saying no. But one extra trip a week to the crick wasn't much more than he was doing already. And if it'd make Ma happy . . .

"Flowers would be kind of pretty out there," he said. "What kind were you thinking of, Ma?"

"Some morning glories and a rosebush or two," she said. "And maybe you could make a fence, Adam. For the flowers to climb on."

"Now hold on," said Adam in mock sternness. "Flowers are one thing, but a fence is another. Especially if I've got to make it."

"Well, if you don't think . . ."

"I was just joshing you, Ma," said Adam with a chuckle. "I'll make your fence, first thing tomorrow. It won't take any time at all."

By the time the chores were done after supper, Adam was bone tired. He went to bed early. But his shoulders ached from scooping water, and he just couldn't fall asleep. He punched his pillow angrily. He and Ma and Pa worked hard on the farm. It was a shame they could barely scratch out a living. All because they had no water!

He tossed and turned in bed, staring first at the little table in the corner and then out the open window, where the full moon was just clearing the horizon, and finally at the open door of his closet.

A ray of moonlight came through the window, and the closet door seemed to glow in the dark. There, hanging on a hook, were the pants he'd worn to the Church Social yesterday.

The Church Social—Thaddeus Blinn. What had the sign said?

I can give you whatever you ask for.

"I don't think you can deliver on this one, Mr. Thaddeus Blinn," Adam whispered into the still air. "But where's the harm in trying?"

He got out of bed, walked barefoot to the closet, and searched through the pants pockets. There, all crumpled and wrinkled, was the card with the red spot. Smoothing it as best he could against the back of the door, Adam pressed his thumb against the spot.

"I wish . . ." he began. "I wish we had water

all over this farm. Enough for washing and cooking and drinking and for the crops, and . . . and with plenty to spare, too!"

He felt his thumb grow warm against the spot and dropped the card to the floor. He went to the window and looked out. Everything seemed as it had always been. He listened. No sound of gurgling water.

"I guess my wish is too much even for the great Wish Giver," he said glumly as he got back into bed. "No water. Tarnation!"

When Adam woke up Tuesday morning, his first thought was that he didn't have to go to school until the end of the week, when tests began.

Then he remembered the wish he'd made last night. He dressed quickly, gulped his breakfast, and rushed outside to see if maybe . . .

The sun hung in the sky like a big shiny brass disc, and the yard around the house was cracked and dusty from lack of water. "I guess my wish ain't going to come true," he murmured to himself.

"What wish, Adam?" There was Ma, back from the barn with an empty feed dish in her hand.

"Nothing, Ma. Now where was it you wanted your fence set up?" Adam was flustered that

Ma'd heard his talk about wishing. He was too old for such nonsense.

"Just here under the window," Ma replied. "No, the house will shade it from the afternoon sun. Perhaps there by . . . or maybe off to the side where it can be seen from the porch. . . . Then again, it could go . . . oh, I don't know, Adam. Where do you think it should go?"

Adam grinned and shook his head. It did beat all, the trouble Ma had making up her mind when she was doing something to please herself. She could spend an hour just deciding whether to pay a visit to her neighbor, Mrs. Jenks, and when it came to choosing fabric for a new dress, she'd stand in Stew Meat's store all morning, sorting through the bolts of cloth until she found one that was exactly right.

But running the farm was another thing altogether. "Edward, you get the horses to the blacksmith before you do another thing," she'd tell Pa, like a general giving orders. Or, "Adam, the beans need cultivating. Right now!" And Pa and Adam would obey, figuring Ma was seldom wrong about when farm work had to get done.

Adam knew how to get Ma to make up her mind. "Why don't you put the fence over there?"

he said, pointing to the one spot that didn't get any sun all day long.

"Oh, you men!" Ma answered. "Any fool can see the best spot is there on the corner, where we can see the flowers from two sides of the house. That'll do nicely." She picked up Uncle Poot's dowsing rod from where Adam had dropped it and scratched a line in the dusty earth.

Adam paced the length of the line. He calculated that five fence posts would do, and he scuffed the dirt with his heel at the places he'd dig them.

He made the five holes with a spade. Each hole was about two feet deep. "You're making too much work for yourself, Adam," Ma told him. "Are you trying to go all the way down to China?"

"I want them posts to stay put," Adam said. "Not blowing over in the first strong wind." The earth at the bottom of each hole was as dry as that on the surface. If the whole farm was like that, it'd be a bad year for the crops unless they got watered soon. He'd have to make another trip to Spider Crick after lunch.

Adam leaned on the spade, resting. He looked about the dusty yard and down toward the hollow where the barn was. Then his eyes lit on the dowsing rod.

He picked it up. Just a thin, two-pronged branch of applewood, he thought. How had Uncle Poot held it?

He bent his arms at the elbows and gripped a prong in each upturned palm. The small stub of wood at the crotch stuck out ahead as if pointing the way to go. Adam took one step. Another.

Suddenly the prongs started twisting and turning in Adam's hands like live things. The pointer jerked straight down, and the branch's bark wrinkled and split as the dowsing rod bent into an arc.

Adam tried yanking up against whatever force was pulling on the stick. It was impossible. The stick had a life of its own, and it insisted on pointing to the soil at Adam's feet.

Adam loosed his grip on the dowsing rod, and it dropped to the ground. There it lay, no longer curved, but just a forked stick from an ordinary apple tree. Adam was scared stiff.

Gingerly he picked up the dowsing rod. Hot as the day was, he could feel cold sweat on his forehead. He walked to the other end of the yard.

140

Again he grasped the two prongs of the stick, just as he'd seen Uncle Poot do it. He took a single step forward.

Once more the pointer jerked toward the ground, almost as if an invisible hand had reached out of the earth and pulled at it. Adam could feel the skin on his hands being rubbed raw. With a mighty effort he hurled the stick from him, watching it turn into a lifeless bit of wood in midair.

Uncle Poot's words popped into Adam's head: "When I walk over an underground stream holding the prongs of my dowsing rod, t'other end of it will twist down and point to water like a fish pole when a trout hits the lure."

Adam gasped. He had the dowsing gift himself! Or did he?

The yard all about him was as dry and parched as it had ever been. There couldn't be water under there.

So what had caused the dowsing rod to jerk and point? He decided to try again.

The branch began to twist in his hands as soon as he took his first step with it. He crisscrossed the yard several times. Wherever he went, the stick yanked itself toward the ground like a pointing finger.

"Ma!" Adam dropped the rod and ran pell-mell toward the house. "Ma!"

Mrs. Fiske came to the kitchen door. "What are you howling about, Adam?" she asked. "Are you hurt or something?"

"I think I found water, Ma," Adam crowed. "Water under the whole yard. The dowsing rod points down wherever I go."

"Then why didn't Uncle Poot find it yesterday?" Ma replied with a snort. "All the water on this farm wouldn't give a cricket a good drink. Get inside and put the plates out, Adam. Pa'll be here directly, and he'll be hungry."

"But Ma . . . only water could make the rod bend the way it did," said Adam. "Uncle Poot said so."

"You're talking nonsense, Adam. I think the heat's got to you. Go in the parlor and rest. I'll get things ready here."

"But . . ."

"That's enough. Do as I say."

Adam plodded into the parlor. He wondered how he could get Ma to—

POP

He heard a sound like somebody'd taken a huge cork out of a gigantic bottle. Then there was another sound, this one a wet, liquid hissing.

FSSSHHHHH

Adam heard the sounds a second time.

POP   FSSSHHHHH

And a third! A fourth! A fifth!

POP   FSSSHHHHH

POP   FSSSHHHHH

POP   FSSSHHHHH

Before he even had time to wonder what had caused the strange noises, his mother called loudly. "Adam! Close the windows in there! Heaven be praised, it's starting to rain!"

Through the parlor window, Adam saw the parched yard and the clear blue sky and the fiery ball that was the sun. "It sure ain't raining on this side of the house!" he yelled back.

He still heard the hissing. *FSSSHHHHH*

"Adam, come help me! The curtains are getting soaked!"

He ran to the kitchen. Large drops of water were spattering in through the open window over the sink, and he could hear water drumming onto the roof and gurgling through the gutter pipes on its way to the big cistern in the cellar.

Adam dashed out onto the back porch. He couldn't believe what he saw!

From each of the fence post holes he'd dug, water was gushing forth as if spewed from a fire hose. Up. Up. Higher than the house the silvery liquid spouted, forming five columns that glittered as the sunlight caught them. At the top of each column the water spread out in all directions, so that there appeared to be five watery umbrellas at the corner of the house.

"Water!" Adam cried as he ran under the falling drops. There he stood, getting soaked to the skin and laughing out loud. "Water!"

There was an awed gasp from behind him. Adam turned about.

Pa was gazing at the spouts with wonder in his eyes. Then Ma rushed out of the kitchen. "Never in my life have I seen it rain as hard as—"

She caught sight of the five spurting columns and fell silent, her mouth gaping.

"It's real water," said Pa over the sound of the hissing spouts. "Out there in the cornfield, I

thought I was going soft in the head."

"What happened in the cornfield, Edward?" Ma asked.

"I jabbed a hoe in the ground," Pa replied, "and water started coming out of it. Not just running along the ground, but shooting right up in the air. Like those spouts, but nowhere near as big. I thought I was addled from too much sun or else coming down sick. Anyhow, I poked another hole, and water came up out of *that* one, too. In all my life I never saw the like of it. It can't be happening. It just can't be. . . ."

"But it is!" cried Adam. "We finally got water on this here farm."

"It's more'n a little strange," said Pa. "Still, it'd be a shame not to use what's been provided. I plan on jabbing more holes, so's I can water all the crops. Adam, tote the tubs up here and fill 'em. No telling how long the water will keep spouting."

But the water didn't stop. By the middle of the afternoon all the crops had been given a good drink, and every tub and pot and kettle on the place was filled with water. Runoff from the gutters had filled the big iron cistern in the cellar, and Adam had to unhook the pipe that led inside so the water could run off into the yard.

At bedtime that evening the water was still gushing forth as strong as ever. It hissed from the five holes and pattered loudly on the roof. "I hope that noise won't keep us awake," said Ma.

"The sound of that water is better'n the sweetest music I ever heard," said Pa. "I plan on sleeping like a log tonight."

Adam smiled a sleepy smile as he lay on his bed that night. Water—gurgling in the gutters and spattering to the ground and making the plants grow. No more hauling the tubs down to Spider Crick and filling 'em up and hauling 'em back again. Everything seemed just about as perfect as it could be.

With a contented sigh, he fell asleep.

That night Adam had a dream. He was standing in the icy cold water of Spider Crick, scooping up one bucketful after another as he tried to fill a hundred huge tubs on a wagon as large as the Coven Tree Village Green.

Suddenly something coiled about his ankles. He tried to reach the bank of the crick, but the thing pulled him farther into the dark waters. His legs were jerked viciously. He felt himself falling. Shivering and shaking, he tumbled. . . .

Adam woke up. The morning sun shone through the window, but he still felt cold. The hissing of the waterspouts outside and the rumble of water hitting the roof were almost drowned out by the chattering of Adam's teeth.

Drip . . . drip . . . drip . . . drip . . .

He sat up and looked at the foot of the bed. The blankets there were soaked with water, and the wet cloth was wrapped tightly about his ankles. On the ceiling was a large damp spot. He watched another drop of water collect in the center of the spot and then fall onto the foot of the bed.

The roof was leaking.

Quickly Adam got up. He found a bucket in the broom closet and brought it back to his room. Moving the bed aside, he put the bucket under the drip. As he started to get dressed, the *ting . . . ting* of the falling drops added itself to the sounds of the gushing spouts and the water on the roof.

Ma had oatmeal ready in the kitchen. "There's a leak in the roof," Adam told her as he ate. "Somewhere over my room."

"I wouldn't wonder," said Ma. "The water was spurting out all night. Our roof has had more water on it in a single day than rain would bring in ten years. I couldn't sleep with all the noise."

"Maybe Pa and I could fix the leak," Adam said.

"Your Pa's got other things on his mind. Look."

Adam went to the window. The water from

the spouts had washed out a gully that led down to the hollow where the barn was. The barn looked different now, too. It seemed to sit on a smooth, flat surface that reflected the sunlight in glittering waves.

There was a pool of water down there. The barn was flooded!

"Pa's trying to get the mess cleaned up," said Mrs. Fiske. "You'd best go help him, Adam. If the water doesn't stop soon, I don't know what's to become of us."

Adam pulled on his high boots and then splashed his way to the barn. Pa was standing near the stalls, talking softly to the horses.

The whole floor of the barn was underwater. In one corner, two full sacks of grain were now soggy lumps of mush. The ducks seemed happy enough, paddling about from the stalls to the granary to the threshing floor like a squadron of tiny boats and quacking joyfully. The chickens perched on the edge of the hayloft, where Pa had set them. They ruffled their soaked feathers with furious clucks and generally acted as mad as . . . well, as mad as wet hens.

"First," Pa told Adam, "you take the horses to the Jenks farm while I see if any of the grain is dry enough to be worth saving. Then we'll carry the tools and such up to the hayloft. That's well above the water—at least for now."

The work in the barn took most of the morning. Pa had moved all the dry grain by the time Adam got back from the Jenks farm. The two of them rescued most of the large tools from the steadily rising lake in the barn. But many of the smaller things—chains and snaffles and clevises and such—were lost beneath the water.

"I guess we've done about all we can," said Pa finally. "But those spouts by the house are going as strong as ever, and the water coming out of them holes I poked in the fields doesn't show signs of quitting either. It's surely odd how the water just keeps coming and coming. The whole farm is drenched."

"The crops won't die, will they?" Adam asked fearfully.

"Hard to tell," Pa answered. "Right now they're just getting a good drink. But they'll either be drowned or go rotten if the water doesn't stop soon. It does beat all how the water's just on this place. Once it reaches the end of our land, it just disappears down into the ground."

"But what'll we do if we lose the crops, Pa?"

"We'll make do somehow. Right now I've got more on my mind than a few bushels of corn."

"Like what, Pa?" What could be worse than having all the crops die? Adam wondered.

"Look there, Adam. D'you see all that higher ground around the house and the barn? Our buildings are down in a kind of hollow. And if that hollow fills with water—"

"Pa!" Adam gasped. "We'd be living in the middle of a lake!"

Pa nodded. "If the water doesn't let up in the next day or so, the only thing that'll be comfortable in our front parlor is fish. I figure on staying put as long as possible, but we just might have to leave the farm before we're drowned out."

"Leave the farm, Pa? That'd be awful!"

"We won't have much choice unless the water lets up. And don't carry on so. I bought this farm, and I can buy another. It'll take a few lean years while we save up the money, but we've seen bad times before, and I guess we'll weather this one all right."

Then Pa waved a warning finger. "Not a word to Ma about this, Adam. No sense getting her upset just now. Maybe the water'll stop, and we'll have done all this worrying for nothing."

But as the day wore on, the water kept on gushing up out of the ground. Every few minutes Adam would peek out the kitchen window. The pond around the barn was deeper every time he looked. It crept closer and closer to the house like some hungry monster.

Toward the middle of the afternoon Adam looked out and saw a small knot of people standing on the high ground overlooking the house and barn. "Pa," he said. "Folks are coming out from town to see what's going on."

"I reckon I'd do the same if I was one of them," said Pa in a tired voice. "Go out and see 'em if you like, Adam. I'm weary from all that work this morning. I'll just sit here and keep myself company."

Adam wanted to find out what other people thought about the spouting water. As he walked up the hill to the high ground, he heard Jonas Colby, the stationmaster, arguing loudly with Wilbur Baldwin, who taught science at the high school. Mr. Colby was used to winning his arguments.

"Consarn it, Wilbur!" he was saying. "You can talk until you're blue in the face about underground rivers and rock strata and all that rubbish. But how in tarnation do you explain them things?" He poked a finger in the direction of the five spouts.

"Wells . . . called artesian wells . . . sometimes come up . . ." began Mr. Baldwin.

"I don't give a hoot if every artist in the world has got a well," interrupted Mr. Colby with a cackling laugh. "There's nothing in any of your almighty science books to explain how water can be shooting up out of the ground like that. Admit it. Here's one thing you don't know beans about."

"No, I don't," replied Mr. Baldwin. "But that doesn't mean—"

"Maybe we're just seeing things, huh? Maybe them things ain't really there, flooding out the barn." Then Mr. Colby dug his elbow playfully into Mr. Baldwin's ribs. "Or how about this, Wilbur—maybe it's magic!"

At the word *magic*, Adam's stomach seemed to turn to jelly. The Church Social . . . Thaddeus Blinn . . . the wish card . . . He remembered all of these. Just as clearly, he suddenly remembered his own wish:

I wish we had water all over this farm.

"All over this farm"—that's what he'd said. But he'd only meant—

"Adam?"

It was Sven Hensen, the blacksmith. Sven was more than six feet tall, and as thick and hard as a full-grown oak tree. Once Adam had seen him lift two steel anvils off the ground without even sweating.

"Iss all dat water givin' you and your pa trouble, Adam?" Sven asked.

Adam nodded his head.

"You vant I should cap dem spouts so you don't get no more water?"

"Could you really do that, Mr. Hensen?" Adam couldn't believe there was a way to turn the spouts off.

"Sure. I show you." Sven took mighty strides toward the house, with Adam trotting close behind. The blacksmith found a washtub on the back porch. "Dis'll do joost fine," he said.

Sven walked to the nearest spouting column, paying no attention to the water that was pouring down on him. He lifted the tub high above his head.

"YAAAHHHHH!" Sven's shout rang in Adam's

ears as the blacksmith brought the tub down over the spout. He leaped onto the tub's bottom and raised both hands above his head.

"Look there!" called somebody on the hill. "Sven Hensen has capped the first spout!"

Now there were only four columns of water. "Come, you people!" Sven ordered. "You drive stakes deep in ground around tub. Den you tie down tub with rope and . . . Ohhhhhh!"

Before anyone could obey, a rumbling came from deep underground. Sven, still standing on the tub, began to rise into the air. Water shot out of the ground, pushing the tub higher. The blacksmith was above the porch roof before the tub slid off the column of water. Both Sven and the tub came crashing back to earth with a thud and a clang.

"Mr. Hensen!" cried Adam in alarm. "Are you all right?"

Sven sat up, looked about, shook his head, and got to his feet.

"I joost get wind knocked out from me," he said. "But dat water's powerful strong, Adam. I'm strongest man in Coven Tree. If I can't put cap on dem spouts, nobody else can do it neither."

Sadly, Adam made his way back to the house. For the rest of that day, he and Ma and Pa sat without saying a word, simply watching the water come closer and closer. They all knew the farm was as good as lost. But nobody wanted to talk about it.

By suppertime, Adam had worked up his courage to tell Pa about the terrible wish he'd made. "Pa," he began, "when I was at the Church Social last Saturday, I saw a little man in a white suit. He told me . . ."

"Adam, be still!" ordered his mother sharply. "Your pa's in no mood to hear about your frivolous goings-on."

"But Ma, I—"

"That's enough, Adam!" Ma whacked his wrist hard with her teaspoon. Adam couldn't remember another time when Ma had struck him in anger.

"I'll be quiet, Ma," he said in a whisper.

Later, as he was getting ready for bed, Adam heard a new noise above the hissing of the spouts and the drumming on the roof and the *tink-tink* of the drip from the ceiling. It was water, running and trickling as if into a still pool. But the sound was coming from just underneath the floor on which his bed sat.

Pa appeared at the door of his room, holding a lantern.

"The water's reached the cellar windows," he told Adam. "It's coming inside now. Tomorrow we'll have to move out."

When Adam got up Thursday morning, he looked out the window first thing. There was a big lake all around the house, lapping against the foundation. Much of the barn was underwater. The five spouts were gushing as strong as ever, and the drumming sound on the roof was loud in Adam's ears.

Quickly he pulled on his clothes and went into the kitchen. The roof there was leaking now—leaking badly. Pails and pots and pans were all over the floor, each one catching its own drip from the ceiling. Ma stood at the stove. She was wearing her black rubber raincoat and hat, and in one hand she held an open umbrella. With the other she flipped an egg in the skillet. A drop of water hit the umbrella, rolled off, and hissed as it hit the hot stove.

"You shouldn't be cooking this morning," Adam told her. "We could get along without breakfast this once."

"I've cooked breakfast at this stove every day since your pa built this house," she replied. "I'm not about to give it up now, even if it is our last day here."

In her own way, thought Adam, Ma could be just as stubborn as Pa.

"Ahoy, the house!" Adam heard Pa cry from somewhere outside. "Ready yourselves. Captain Fiske is coming into harbor!"

Ma threw open the back door, and Adam saw a sight stranger than he'd ever expected. There was Pa, soaked to the skin, standing on what looked to be some kind of a raft. The frame was heavy wooden beams, notched at odd places. Underneath, a barrel was fastened at each corner to make the craft float high in the water, and the whole thing was tied together with cords, baling wire, and heavy ropes. Pa stood at the rear with a long pole in his hands, using it to push the raft ahead.

"This here's parts of the chickenhouse and the horse stalls," he said. "I had to tear apart a few things down in the barn to get what I needed."

"It . . . it's a fine raft, Pa," said Adam.

"The water'll rise and flood the first floor in a few hours," said Pa. "We'll have to raft the furniture and such to high ground while there's still time." He pointed toward where a little hill marked the beginning of the Jenks farm.

"Before we start," said Adam, "let me tell you about the wish . . . and the little man at the Church Social . . . and—"

"No time for idle chitchat now, Adam," said Pa. "The water's coming up fast, and we've got to get a move on. I'll sail this thing around to the front, where those spouts won't be dropping water on us. You go through the parlor and unlock the door for me. Toot! Toot!" Pa pretended to pull on the rope of a boat whistle.

"How that man can make jokes at a time like this is beyond me," Ma told Adam.

He opened the front door just as Pa poled his way around the corner of the house. Pa threw Adam a rope, and between them they soon had the raft bobbing just outside the door.

"The davenport goes first," Pa said. "And maybe one of those straight chairs. We can't put too much on at once or we'll capsize."

He and Adam loaded the raft, and off they floated toward the hill. Once ashore, they unloaded and began poling back for a second load. It was slow going, with the raft wallowing in the water like a tired walrus.

The beds took two trips, and once Pa's overstuffed chair almost slid into the water. They took Ma herself over to the hill in the middle of a load of pots and pans and knickknacks. Back and forth they went for hours. Finally, the only thing left was the big cookstove in the kitchen.

Adam gripped the stovepipe where it went through the wall and twisted. As the pipe came loose, a cloud of soot poured down over his head and shoulders.

"Phooo!" Adam snorted. "Pa, I'm covered with—"

"You can wash later," Pa told him. "There's water aplenty. Right now we've got to get this stove out of here."

The stove was heavier than anything else in the house, and Adam had all he could do to carry his end. Just as they got it on board the raft, they heard a loud *SLUUUSH* as the rising water came in through the front door and up from the cellar, covering the floorboards.

163

"The house is sinking!" cried Pa. "Shove off, Adam."

They were still some twenty feet from the hill that marked the beginning of dry land when . . .

CRACK

"What's that, Pa?" whispered Adam in a frightened voice.

"I don't know. It . . ."

CRACK

"The raft's breaking up!" Adam cried. "The stove's too heavy. Faster, Pa! Faster!"

They both pushed harder with their poles, but it was too late.

CRACK CRUNCH

The whole raft came apart. The stove broke through the deck and sank like a rock. The side of the raft tipped up, dumping Adam and Pa into the cold water.

"Swim, Edward!" called Ma from shore. "Adam, swim! Swim for your lives. You can't drown now. Help, somebody. Help!"

"Sarah, will you stop that caterwauling?" yelled Pa. His roars of laughter rang out across the water. "The water here only comes up to our waists."

By the time the household goods had been arranged on shore, two or three wagons were coming up the road from town. The good folks of Coven Tree weren't about to stand by idly when a neighbor was in trouble. Whole families began arriving. The men and boys offered help in moving the furniture away from the shore of the lake, and the women and girls brought food enough for an army and offers of spare rooms where the Fiskes could stay.

But Pa would have none of it. "We'll just camp out here," he told Mayor Tubbs. "A little hard luck ain't going to make us lose heart. A man ain't licked until he hollers 'uncle.'"

"But it'll be dark soon," said the mayor. "Isn't there anything we can do?"

"Yes, sir, there is. I'd be obliged if you'd just leave us alone for a bit to sort things out."

The villagers left then. As the sun settled down on the western horizon, the Fiskes were alone at the edge of the lake that had once been their farm. Pa built a small fire and opened a can of beans with the axe. Ma spread blankets on the ground to sit on as they ate. The only sounds were the hissing of the waterspouts and the patter of water on flooded fields.

Adam took a deep breath. "Pa?"

"What?"

"It was me, Pa. I'm the one who done it!"

"Done what, Adam?"

Adam began his story. He told of the Church Social and Thaddeus Blinn and the card and the wish he'd made and what that wish had turned into. When he finished he sat silently, waiting for Pa to roar out his anger or thrash him with a stick or . . . or . . .

"It don't seem possible," murmured Pa softly.

He walked to the shore and dabbled the toe of one shoe in the water. "It don't seem possible," he repeated. "I never thought to see something like this in a dozen lifetimes . . . and all from one little wish. Still, it's happening. So it must be magic."

"Ain't—ain't you going to get mad, Pa?" Adam asked.

"Because you made a wish, Adam?" Pa replied. "I must have made the same wish a hundred times in years past. The only difference was, I didn't have the card with the red spot. But if I'd had it, I'd have used it, same as you. No, Adam, I'm sad that our farm is gone. But I'm not angry with you. Wishing that things were better is something all people do."

Adam felt a sense of relief wash over him. It was good to have the whole story out in the open, and not bottled up inside anymore. And Pa . . . Pa wasn't even angry with him.

It was quite dark now, and as Adam looked up the valley he saw a light go on at the Jenks farm. And another light at the Bingham place. Then the watchman at the sawmill put a lantern in the window, and a soft glow from Doc Rush's office showed he was working late.

Four lights—four little spots in the darkness.

Suddenly Adam got to his feet. "Four!" he whispered. "There's four!"

"We see the lights, too," his mother answered. "But what—"

"I have something I have to be doing," said Adam, his voice quivering with excitement. "I won't be long. Pa . . . Ma . . . you wait right here."

"Adam, where are you off to?" Pa asked.

But there was no answer. For by then Adam was running with long strides around the edge of the lake and toward the road that led into Coven Tree.

At Stew Meat's Store

H

Hello. It's me again— Stew Meat.

As you've seen, within a few short days after they'd accepted those cards from Thaddeus Blinn, all three of those young folks—Polly Kemp and Rowena Jervis and Adam Fiske—had gotten themselves into deep trouble. Oh, maybe they'd learned a few things from what had happened when they'd wished unwisely, but I'd rather tell my story and leave the teaching to others. Let's just say they all paid a high price indeed for having their wishes come true.

Polly couldn't say a harsh word to anyone, no matter how necessary it was to speak out, without *jug-a-rum*ing like a bullfrog for the next half hour or so. Rowena had a stubby sycamore tree in the grove out back of her place, and in the knots and scars on its trunk she could still see the terror-filled face of Henry Piper. And Adam Fiske and his family were without a home now that the house and barn were flooded and the whole farm had water pelting down on it.

But as hopeless as their plights seemed, I guess for every problem there's a solution of some kind. And that's what brings me back into the story again.

It was Thursday evening following the Saturday of the Church Social. I've found it's good business to keep my store open late toward the end of the week so the farmers roundabout can buy in the evenings what they haven't time to shop for during the day. And even at nine o'clock I have to shoo the hangers-on out into the street so I can lock up and balance my ledgers.

I'd just closed the big front door after Dan'l and Jenny Pitt and was about to slide the bolt home when I heard a sound behind me. I turned around to see who it was.

There was Polly Kemp, peering out from behind a hardware display in the far corner.

I opened my mouth to tell her to skedaddle, but before I could get a word out, the front door banged open again, and in rushed Rowena Jervis.

Right behind her was somebody else, too. Adam Fiske, of course, panting and gasping for breath like he'd run all the way from Boston.

"What in tarnation are you three doing here after hours?" I asked. I was annoyed, no two ways about it. It had been a long day, and I was tired.

Still, in the past half week or so I'd heard and seen some mighty strange happenings that involved those three. So my annoyance was tempered by curiosity.

"I . . . I have to see you, Stew Meat," said Rowena nervously. "It's awful important."

"Me too," said Adam. "It just can't wait."

"But I was here first," snapped Polly. "Who do you two think you are, coming in here and . . . ?" Then she gave a little shake of her head and closed her mouth right quick.

"The three of you, all wanting me?" I asked. "Can't it wait until tomorrow morning?"

"No!" All three of 'em cried out like they were singing in chorus, and I knew it had to be something serious. So I had 'em sit down on crates while I took the old swivel chair by the stove.

"Now then," I said. "What is it?"

With that, they all began talking at once, waving their hands in the air and each one trying to outshout the others.

"Hold it!" I bellowed. "Let's get organized. Polly, you first. Then Rowena. And then Adam."

So they told me their stories—just the way they're set down here.

When they'd all finished, there wasn't a more astonished man in the world than I was. I'd been dead wrong in laughing at the things Thaddeus Blinn had claimed. The Wish Giver could make dreams come true. But only on his own terms, of course.

"That Thaddeus Blinn," I growled. "I should have known right off the kind of a creature he was. I thought there was something strange about his eyes. He was as evil as any witch or imp that ever came through these parts.

"But what do you want from me?" I asked finally. "I'm no wish giver."

All three of 'em looked at one another for a moment. At length Rowena Jervis spoke up.

"Do you still have the card?" she asked me. "The one with the red spot?"

I nodded.

"You haven't made a wish on it yet, have you?" Polly added.

Then it was clear to me. I was the only way they had of getting free of the trouble they'd made for themselves. I went to the cash register and pressed the No Sale lever. With a *bong* the drawer slid open. I reached way into the back. Amid a pile of bills and credit slips I found the card from Thaddeus Blinn.

"Now, Stew Meat," Rowena said, "if you'd just press your thumb against the spot and say something like 'I wish Henry Piper was a man again,' I'd be ever so grateful."

"Wait a minute!" cried Adam. "That big pond on our farm has got to—"

"Rowena Jervis, you are a selfish, inconsiderate lout!" yelled Polly at the same time. "And I think you ought to—

"JUG-A-RUM!"

At the sound of the frog's croak, Adam and Rowena quieted down and just stared at Polly, who was clutching her throat. That allowed me to get a word in.

"You three are forgetting something," I told them. "According to Thaddeus Blinn, I can use this card to wish for anything—anything at all. And I plan on making my wish right now."

"But the water . . ." exclaimed Adam.

"Henry Piper . . ." Rowena put in.

"JUG-A-RUM!" added Polly.

I took the card in my right hand and pressed my thumb against the red spot. The store got all quiet then, with the three of 'em staring at the card as if it were a live thing that might bite.

"I wish . . ." I said. "Now I have to get this just right . . . I wish that all three of these young 'uns will have their wishes canceled out this very minute. And Mr. Blinn, I don't want any of the misery that usually comes with such wishing, either."

I felt the spot on the card grow warm—almost hot—beneath my thumb. At the same time those three all began jawing at one another again. And of course Polly Kemp was the loudest.

*"JUG-A-RUM! JUG-A-RUM! JUG-A-RR*rrreally think it'll work, do you? I'm gonna be stuck for all time croaking like . . ."

I never saw a more excited girl in my life. "I—I can talk again!" she cried joyfully. "It's only

been a couple of minutes since I said . . . And now I can talk!"

Then she turned to me. " 'Scuse me, Stew Meat," she said. "But I've got to see if the spell's really broken. Now, I think you are the low-downest, cheatingest, short-weightingest old skinflint who ever lived in Coven Tree. And you are shiftless and no-account and . . . and . . . and oh, Stew Meat, I didn't mean any of them things I said to you, but I had to see if I was over that croaking business. Thank you, Stew Meat. Oh, thank you!"

And with that she gave me a big kiss right on the cheek.

We found out later that at just the same time Polly Kemp was calling me all those names, Rowena Jervis's father and mother were sitting out on their back porch. Suddenly they heard a shout from the grove of trees at the far end of the yard, and then the sound of running footsteps. Mr. Jervis took up a lantern and went out to see who it was, but when he entered the trees he found nobody—just a scrap of paper on the ground. It was an order blank.

NEVERFAIL FARM IMPLEMENT COMPANY

—HENRY PIPER, SALESMAN—

———

And by the big pond that was his farm, Edward Fiske stood up and peered into the darkness. "Sarah!" he called to his wife. "Listen to that."

"I don't hear anything," she replied in a sleepy voice.

"That's just it—there's nothing to hear. The spouts of water have stopped."

Well, maybe some good did come of the wish cards after all. Polly Kemp spends a lot more of her time saying what she likes about people rather than what's wrong with them—though she can still be pretty blunt with anyone who gets her dander up. She's got a lot more friends in school now, too, and the Wickstaff twins haven't dropped a snake down her back or thrown her in the crick for nearly three months.

Sam Waxman took Rowena Jervis to the husking bee this fall, and she's stitching him a quilt with a Cupid's bow design. And sometimes at meals, when they think nobody's looking, the two of 'em hold hands under the table. Mr. Jervis says the way those two carry on, it's enough to make a body sick to his stomach. But he smiles when he says it.

Adam Fiske? Well, the farm was a dead loss,

more's the pity. Once all that water soaked into the ground again, the place went back to being as dry as it ever was. Not a place to grow crops, that's for sure.

But the Fiskes don't care. Adam's got himself a new calling that pays a lot better'n that ol' farm ever did. He really does have the gift for being a dowser man, and now he and Uncle Poot are in business together, going throughout the county and locating water with forked sticks. Dowsing pays pretty well around these parts, and next year when Ed and Sarah Fiske start in to farming again, Adam'll be able to buy 'em a place they can be proud of.

And that's about all there is to my story. So I'll end now, leaving you with just this one thought:

As far as I know, Thaddeus Blinn is still out there, roaming the highways and byways of this land of ours. So if you're ever at a carnival or a fair or a community social and you meet a little fat man in a white suit, with a thick watch chain across his red vest . . . have a care!

Look closely at his eyes.

Especially if he tells you he can give you anything you ask for.

Before you take him up on his offer, think it over. Think very carefully.

Maybe there's something else you'd rather spend fifty cents on.

THE END